MILLIPEDES
AND MOON TIGERS

MILLIPEDES
AND MOON TIGERS
Science and Policy
in an Age of Extinction

Steve Nash

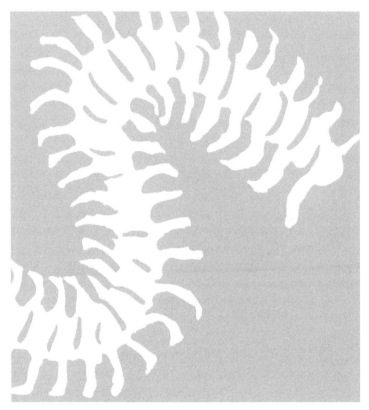

University of Virginia Press
Charlottesville and London

University of Virginia Press
© 2007 by the Rector and Visitors of the University of Virginia
All rights reserved
Printed in the United States of America on acid-free paper

First published 2007

9 8 7 6 5 4 3 2 1

Library of Congress Cataloging-in-Publication Data

. Nash, Steve, 1947–
   Millipedes and moon tigers : science and policy in an age of
extinction / Steve Nash.
        p.   cm.
   Includes index.
   ISBN-13: 978-0-8139-2623-0 (acid-free paper)
   1. Environmental policy—United States. 2. Science and state—
United States. 3. Scientists—United States—Political activity. 4. United
States—Environmental conditions. 5. Environmental protection—
United States. 6. Nature—Effect of human beings on—United States.
7. Landscape—Social aspects—United States. 8. Natural areas—United
States. 9. Historic sites—Conservation and restoration—United States.
10. United States—History, Local. I. Title.
   GE180.N27 2007
   333.72—dc22

                                                              2006025466

FOR LOUISE BRIGGS
AND FOR LOWELL NASH

Contents

Acknowledgments

Journalists always depend on the good will, trust, and patience of the people they rely on for information, and we must hope that those sources feel their confidence has not been betrayed. My reporting has absorbed the attention and energy, not to mention the time, of dozens of people, especially those who have trekked through forests or laboratories to show me their work. They are usually far busier than their willingness to endure my questions would indicate. I am ever in their debt, but I claim all errors that may have crept into this work as my own.

The University of Richmond, where I teach, has provided career-long support and encouragement for my writing. My wife, Linda, has shared my enthusiasm for the natural world and abided my sometimes obscure writing pursuits, and has been my chief enabler on all counts. My Aunt Louise has been a loyal reader and West Coast environmental correspondent and has cheered me on over many years. I am deeply grateful to them all.

Substantially similar versions of all chapters of this book except the first have appeared in a variety of newspapers and magazines, listed below. Permission to reprint them is gratefully acknowledged: "Long Road Back" originally appeared as "A Man and His Tree" in the *Washington Post Sunday Magazine,* July 25, 2004; "Small Books, Old Stories" originally appeared as "Seeds of Time" in *Archaeology Magazine* (www.archaeology

.org), a publication of the Archaeological Institute of America (57, no. 1 [January/February 2004]); "Last Stand" originally appeared as "Last Stand: Are Old Growth Forests Worth Saving?" in the *Washington Post Sunday Magazine,* May 25, 2003; "Memory Blanks: Notes on a New Civil War Campaign" originally appeared as "Battles over Battlefields: The Fight to Save Civil War Sites from Developers" in *Archaeology Magazine* (www.archaeology.org), a publication of the Archaeological Institute of America (57, no. 5 [September/October 2004]); "Rough Mountain, & Associates" originally appeared as "Wilderness Areas: Studies in Solitude" in the *Washington Post,* July 28, 1988; "Wolves of Isle Royale" originally appeared as "The Wolves of Isle Royale" in *National Parks* (January/February 1989); "The Songbird Connection" originally appeared under the same title in *National Parks* (November/December 1990); "Mallows, Marking Time" originally appeared as "State's Rarest Plant—All Three Wild Ones—Suffering" in the *Richmond Times-Dispatch and News Leader,* August 30, 1987; "Desperately Seeking Charisma" originally appeared as "Desperately Seeking Charisma: Improving the Status of Invertebrates" in *BioScience* 54, no. 6 (June 2004); "Agroterror" originally appeared as "Assessing the Threat of Agroterror" in the *Scientist* 18, no. 9 (May 10, 2004); "Invasion of the Buggy Snackers (and Other Horrors)" originally appeared under the same title in the *Washington Post,* Sunday, April 11, 2004; "Swimming under the Radar" originally appeared as "Glofish Gives New Shine to GM Debate—Researchers Surprised by Lack of Federal Oversight in Genetically Modified Pet Fish" in the *Scientist* 18, no. 2 (February 2, 2004); "Clones in the Cathedral" originally appeared as "The Phantom Forest: Research on Gene-Altered Trees Leaps Ahead, into Regulatory Limbo" in *BioScience* 53, no. 5 (May 2003); and "Conservation Genetics I" and "Conservation Genetics II" appeared as "New Tools, Moon Tigers, and the Extinction Crisis: Biotechnology, Genetics, Conservation Biology Are Not Always Easy Partners" in *BioScience* 51, no. 9 (September 2001).

Introduction

This book is about how science is being used to help protect essential parts of our rapidly transforming landscapes: their wild species and habitats, their human history. It also records how science is sometimes ignored and the significance of those landscapes is put at risk, or obliterated.

The chapters proceed in a rough chronological order, beginning with drifting continental plates, 50 million years back, and the fate of the American chestnut, and continuing into archaeologist Naomi Miller's sector of deep time several millennia ago when primordial forests were disappearing—sometimes with dire effects—from the Near East.

The tentative survival of the southeastern United States' rare remaining old-growth forests, which predate the European era in North America, is addressed next, followed by a status report on the conflict over preserving an important part of our cultural record—the Civil War battle sites—on the land. History, like endangered species, can be extinguished.

Then comes a mosaic of stories and opinion pieces about environmental issues now facing our remaining natural areas. Finally, some glimpses into the future: the engineered organisms that are already making their way out of their natal laboratories around the country, and onto the landscape.

I like the way Naomi Miller, an environmental archaeologist who appears in this book, makes the case for scientific curiosity as it relates to her own work: "The social value of archaeology," she says, "is putting people in their place—giving them

a sense that we are one little part of a very long continuum. It
. . . is to teach humility—and that we should pay attention."
In her research, that means attending sharply to some of the
particulars of a place's ancient natural history, and how they
intertwine with its record of human culture. Revealing, that is
to say, as much as we can discover about the true identity of
the landscape.

If my reporting over nearly two decades in this collection of
articles finds its mark at least some of the time, it will suggest
the importance of a "sense of place" of this broader kind—a
sense of our changing natural and cultural heritage. May you
find reason in these pages, too, to value the science that dis-
covers, monitors, and predicts such changes, and sometimes
helps to ease their ill effects.

MILLIPEDES
AND MOON TIGERS

Bearings

The middle of nowhere is at 36.1283 degrees north latitude, 77.7946 degrees west longitude, next to a gas-and-snacks place along an interstate highway in rural North Carolina. I spotted it recently and emerged from the car, unfolding myself into the glare of a June midafternoon.

Out past the dumpsters, the asphalt apron here gives way to an overgrown pasture and a soybean field. The view ahead is nearly as flat and featureless as the parking lot behind.

So the map coordinates are available, beguiling in their precision but ultimately a trifle. As with so many of the landscapes we pass through, the real identity of this scene, its natural and cultural history, is uncomprehended. Because of the intensity and pace of human-made change, and because we move around a lot, we often find ourselves in such settings. They may occupy a few pixels in a satellite view, but they have little discernible past or future. Seemingly, they're the middle of nowhere.

That, of course, is an illusion born of our own haste and distraction. Because if for some reason we're curious about trying to reweave its story line, this place has one. Just now, to take up the most visible strand, its margins are slowly being reclaimed by the progenitive forces of wild seeds and small wild animals. If you could press further, you might inquire of the soil thrown up along the ditch, the ants, or the line of poplars and pines in the distance: what's happened on this land over the past several hundred years or more, and what may happen in the future?

We have urgent reason now for curiosity about such changes. They matter, and not just for other species. After I've found my way back out of the field, the biggest headline on the *USA Today* for sale over at the little snack store says, "The Debate's Over: Globe Is Warming." Indeed, in policy terms, knowing where we are and where we've been is essential as we struggle with decisions about environmental issues.

It nearly goes without saying that not everyone values such knowledge, but it's a point worth dwelling on, because an increasing number of scientists—the kind journalists depend on for books like this one—say that American science has entered a new era. They charge that the infrastructure and credibility of science conducted on behalf of the public interest are increasingly subject to political interference.

Environmentalists, of course, have long since concluded that the future of our natural and historical estate—our national forests, national parks, the Great Lakes, the coastal waters—is being squandered, at times through carelessness, more often by design. But now it's scientists—who typically distance themselves from public political avowals—who are coming forward. They claim that the political administration of the federal government, the custodian of much of that heritage, has accelerated its efforts to halt science research, to distort its findings, and to silence the scientists who expose abuses.

A few recent examples are linked to topics in this book. Marine ecologist Jeremy Jackson of the Scripps Institution of Oceanography, who appears in the chapter on invertebrate conservation, says his research has been strongly buffeted by political interference and harassment. "Unwelcome news about the world we live in has become classified very cleverly as advocacy," Jackson told me. He was chief scientist on a recent project in Panama for the Smithsonian's Tropical Research Institute, which investigated the effects of an oil spill on the marine communities on the Caribbean coast. It was funded by the U.S. Department of the Interior, Jackson said, because of the obvious relevance of that oil spill to the possibility of drilling off the west coast of Florida.

"It was a huge spill," he said. "The Smithsonian Institution had been doing research in the region for a very long time, so there was a large amount of data about the coastal ecosystem. We demonstrated for the first time that corals may die on a massive scale as the consequence of a big oil spill."

As soon as those data were made public, the federal agency "started to nickle-and-dime us to death. We were constantly being looked at to see if we were living up to the exact code of the contract for the research we intended to do, which constituted an enormous administrative burden." The Inspector General's office then investigated Jackson, he said, to see if he had faked the data.

"If we go out and observe the world and what we observe is not what they want to hear, then the way they deal with us now is to say that we're biased advocates for a point of view," Jackson said. "In my opinion, there's no doubt that that's especially true in the Bush administration, which has carried it to absurd levels."

Just for argument's sake, dismiss Jackson, despite his reputation as an eminent research scientist, as a crybaby or an ideologue. Then consider the case of wildlife biologist Andrew Eller, who has spent nearly twenty years as a biologist at the U.S. Fish and Wildlife Service, ten of them working on the recovery program for the endangered Florida panther. The near-miracle of improvement in the survival odds for this animal is chronicled here, in one of the chapters on conservation genetics.

Genetics notwithstanding, the panther's fate also depends on whether our own species affords it enough habitat. Part of Eller's job was to assess proposed new golf courses, roads, houses, and strip malls in fast-growing Florida in terms of whether they would jeopardize panther populations, in a document called a "biological opinion." At one point, he has publicly charged, he was threatened with insubordination if he refused to modify a biological opinion and write instead that "there is a surplus of panthers and that the cumulative effects of habitat loss were of no consequence."

In a formal legal complaint against his own agency, filed jointly with a group called Public Employees for Environmental Responsibility (PEER), Eller claimed that the Fish and Wildlife Service based decisions on data that lacked integrity and objectivity, to justify the approval of new real estate development: It used inflated panther population estimates, survival rates, and reproduction rates, and false assumptions that all adult panthers were breeders, including the old, the young, the isolated, and the unfit.

Eller was fired. A few months later, however, the national director of the Fish and Wildlife Service admitted in a formal letter to Eller that "some of the information you challenged has, over, time, been determined to have limitations," and that "corrections are necessary." He was reinstated, but not to work with Florida panthers. He has been assigned to a wildlife refuge in Kentucky.

Anyone would hope that his case is singular, just a bit of anecdotal evidence that tells us nothing reliable about the big picture. Unfortunately, a great many of the other scientists in that agency don't think so. In fact, their experiences indicate strongly that distortion and political interference are pervasive.

More than 1,400 Fish and Wildlife Service biologists, ecologists, botanists, and other science professionals around the United States were surveyed by the Union of Concerned Scientists and PEER in 2005. More than four hundred responded despite being told not to, even on their own time. Here are some excerpts from the results:

- One in five said they have been "directed to inappropriately exclude or alter technical information from a USFWS scientific document," such as a biological opinion.
- Fifty-six percent knew of cases where "commercial interests have inappropriately induced the reversal or withdrawal

of scientific conclusions or decisions through political intervention."

- More than two out of three staff scientists and nearly nine
out of ten scientist-managers who responded knew of
cases "where U.S. Department of Interior political appointees have injected themselves into" the agency's science
research decisions. A majority said members of Congress
or local politicians had also intervened at times.

- A majority did not "trust USFWS decision makers to make
decisions that will protect species and habitats."

- Nearly one in five said they had "been directed by US-
FWS decision makers to provide incomplete, inaccurate
or misleading information to the public, media or elected
officials."

Science rarely has the last word in environmental policy
making, and researchers routinely acknowledge that their
findings are provisional, fragmentary, and uncertain. Science's
most accurate picture of reality is essential, though, as we try
to balance environmental, economic, and social factors in
public policy.

This information is something like the feedback we get in
various ways while driving: the images in the rear-view mirrors
and the windshield, the data on the gas gauge and the speed-
ometer, and the warnings of the "idiot lights." If we purposely
fog the windows, disable the gauges, ignore the warning signals, and drive hard in what we fervently want to be the right
direction, we court mayhem.

"When you hear the name Florida, the first thing you may
think of is Disney World—that fantasyland where everything
is possible," Eller has said. "But what you may not know is that
there is another purveyor of fantasy in Florida . . . they have
spun this elaborate fairy tale that the Florida panther is not
threatened with extinction."

If wildlife biology is rewritten as a fun-house laugh track to
serve powerful private interests in Florida and elsewhere, we

are cheated of a part of our own identity, a reality-based account-
ing of where we live. It means we are effectively converting
ever-larger landscapes into fantasia—the middle of nowhere.

Scientists associated with other federal agencies have similar
concerns. For example, the research of federal climate scientists has been systematically suppressed or twisted to keep the
reality of global warming—which crops up in several places
in these pages—out of public view. Some of the best publicly
funded research we have analyzes the projected warming and
its impacts, not just on polar bears or Maldives Islanders, but
on our own regions of the United States.

When he resigned in 2005, Rick S. Piltz had spent a decade
in senior positions in the coordinating office of the U.S. Climate Change Science Program. He explains that by law, the
dozen or so federal agencies that support most of our climate
research are supposed to produce a science-based National Assessment of the issue every four years.

The last Assessment was published in 2000. It was the most
comprehensive and authoritative study so far of the potential
consequences of climate change for the United States, Piltz
says, the work of a distinguished national team of scientists
and stakeholders, hailed by the National Research Council—
which advises the government on science matters—as exem-
plary and a significant contribution to public understanding.
It includes an easy-to-read overview and easily understood
graphics that illustrate the predicted impact of warming, region by region.

"The regional aspect of it was very important," Piltz says.
"In the second half of the 1990s the debate had really tended
to become quite sterile. At the congressional hearings, it was
either about the climate models, or something going on up in
the atmosphere, or it was cost-benefit analysis of mitigation
options. It just didn't have any kind of discussion with a real
environmental texture, or any geographic specificity.

"To me, that's what you needed: if climate change happened, what would it mean for the Gulf Coast, for the Pacific Northwest, for the Grain Belt? One of the things that the National Assessment accomplished was to get the issue out of the modeling labs and the economics departments."

But Bush administration political appointees have effectively erased the 2000 report from public consciousness, Piltz says, and no new Assessment had appeared by 2006. Federal science agencies had to bend to political dictation: don't build on the report, don't do another one, don't ever refer to it in program documents. He calls its suppression "absolutely scandalous."

After he resigned, Piltz gave the working draft of other key federal climate science reports to the *New York Times*. They had been doctored in dozens of places by a White House political appointee, Phillip Cooney, whose previous employment had been as an antiregulation lobbyist with the American Petroleum Institute. The intent of these editorial changes was to falsify the reports by creating an exaggerated sense of scientific uncertainty about global warming. In the furor that followed, Cooney left, to take a job at Exxon Mobil.

These practices are part of a pattern that corrupts the science-and-policy process, Piltz says: "I think the Bush administration has politicized the Climate Change Science Program. I think they've done it in such a way as to undermine the ability and integrity of the program. . . . The administration has systematically acted to impede honest communication, to suppress, to restrict scientists' freedom of communication, ignore the reports, and misrepresent the state of scientific evidence. It is clearly politically driven.

"They're entitled to their policy, but they aren't entitled to pressure or intimidate the career professionals of the entire technocracy into altering their work so that it suits White House politics."

The Union of Concerned Scientists has issued a statement that includes the following:

When scientific knowledge has been found to be in conflict with its political goals, the administration has often
manipulated the process through which science enters into
its decisions. This has been done by placing people who are
professionally unqualified or who have clear conflicts of interest in official posts and on scientific advisory committees;
by disbanding existing advisory committees; by censoring
and suppressing reports by the government's own scientists;
and by simply not seeking independent scientific advice. . . .
The administration has sometimes misrepresented scientific
knowledge and misled the public about the implications of
its policies.

Russell Train, head of the Environmental Protection Agency
under presidents Nixon and Ford, has endorsed the statement,
along with Nobel laureates, former federal agency directors, university chairs and presidents. By 2006, more than eight thousand scientists from a wide variety of disciplines had signed it.

Long Road Back

This summer marks a century since the beginning of the end for the American chestnut tree. Or you could argue that the trouble really started about 50 million years ago. Neither possibility is much on the mind of Fred Hebard this morning, as he patrols the hummocky roads of his three chestnut research farms. Of more concern just now: a derelict truck a couple of miles away needs the ministrations of a welding torch, and Annie has, once again, jumped ship.

We're near the hamlet of Meadowview, off Interstate 81, on the southwestern big toe of the ragged-foot profile of Virginia. This has also become an evolutionary intersection, though, a place where prosaic small-scale tree farming meets global natural history.

That's because the landscape here—and wherever you live, too—used to be found at a different address. It was part of the supercontinent Laurasia, which combined the land masses of what are now North America and Eurasia. And the remote ancestors of Hebard's chestnut trees grew on Laurasia: their fossil remains have been found along Yellowstone's Specimen Ridge.

But then North America and Eurasia slid off in different directions, and the Atlantic widened between them. The last of the land connecting us with Europe vanished about 50 million years back. To the west, our link with Asia was gone by 15 million years ago. Since then, chestnut trees and thousands of other kinds of plants, though still related, have developed along diverging paths on their separated continents.

This has ramifying consequences, and here's one: some Asian insects and diseases affect trees over there only mildly, since they have shared the same landscape for eons and adapted to each other. Set loose as strangers among distant-cousin trees here in North America, however, those same pests can be lethal.

So when people began to ship Chinese chestnut nursery stock and logs into the United States in the late 1800s, it was as if a bridge had been built, reuniting the two continents. A blight fungus, unanticipated in the evolutionary playbook of American chestnut trees, also crossed over.

The first scientific confirmation of the invading organism was made a hundred summers ago, when it was discovered silently killing trees along the broad avenues of what is now the Bronx Zoo. The vivid orange blight leapt like sparks through stands of chestnuts from Maine to Georgia, consuming an estimated 3.5 billion trees in only fifty years—perhaps a quarter of the entire Appalachian forest.

The same morose scenario—a carelessness akin to arson— has played out again and again since then. Other alien tree-killers continue to make landfall on a regular basis. Fraser firs and butternuts are nearing extinction in the wild; dogwoods and two species of hemlocks have been devastated; ash trees, oaks, and maples and a lengthening list of other kinds of trees are under threat, as imported insects and diseases expand their territory. The scientific outlook: unless Americans decide to take action, more such problems are on the way.

We pull in for gas at Brantley's-N-Dillow's crossroads laundry-grocery—also, biscuits-n-gravy, 99 cents—as a vinyl banner strapped to the cinder blocks announces.

Predictably, everyone hailed in the chance meetings around here seems to be first-names with everyone else. Fred Hebard is no exception, having tooled along these roads, after all, since 1989. He pays up, at a cash register flanked by a display stand with twenty-two different kinds of chewing tobacco.

We need to keep an eye out for the venturesome Annie, a

border collie mix with irrepressible energy. She is, Hebard has explained, a real farm dog: she can jump into the bed of the pickup truck with the tailgate up. That skill works the other way too, though, so she is frequently AWOL. Here she comes back again—"Wag your tail if you're stupid!" is Hebard's affectionate greeting—and we're on our way.

Hebard is a graying, wiry fifty-six, strong enough to wrestle the big, balky driveshaft of a mowing machine onto the back end of a tractor. It's one element of the campaign to contain the explosion of spring weeds across his fields.

And that, in turn, is a little part of Hebard's larger work on behalf of the chestnut tree. On seventy-eight acres, he is trying to reinvent healthy, blight-resistant American chestnut trees and reintroduce them to their original range. To push the continents back apart. Burn the bridge. Leverage the wit and sentiment of *Homo sapiens* against the blind reproductive rapacity of the blight.

Or you could look at it that way. Hebard, a Ph.D. plant disease specialist of modest bearing and entrenched wryness, would wave off any such exalted stuff. "One of my great revelations was when I got poked in the eye by a chestnut twig," he says. "It was that they didn't give a shit that I was trying to help them."

He has, however, a bit of cross-grain fascination with the enemy species: "It just kills the hell out of the chestnut forest. I know it's kind of like admiring the Boston strangler or something," Hebard laughs, "but it's more like a neutral admiration."

In any case, bringing American chestnut trees back isn't a lone-hero project. Instead, it's a mix of scientists, volunteers, long patience, and strong hopes.

Meadowview proper is a short drive from the gas station. Its business section is just a few blocks long, tidy but half-abandoned. There's a phalanx of pickup trucks at the town eatery, where we stop to check in with a couple of other local chestnut experts, the kind whose knowledge of the species is becoming rare. Over grilled cheese and fried potato nuggets, Jack Wilkinson, eighty-eight, remembers that in his childhood "there was mountains of chestnuts. My granddaddy had I guess about fifty acres. We used to say that chestnut was all that was on them. My other granddaddy, he had some. All the big woods had chestnuts in them." When phone lines reached here, to the Holston Valley, chestnut trees supplied the poles. "They was as straight as could be," Wilkinson says, "the healthiest tree in the woods," and one of the most beautiful.

By then, the 1920s, the blight was already bearing down on Meadowview. News reports cited theories that "the real cause is the general wickedness of the people of the United States. It is a scourge for sinfulness and extravagant living. . . . A grand religious revival might stay it." But the flanks of the mountain valleys near Meadowview still had stands of chestnut trees so dense that their heavy load of blossoms was sometimes called "June snow."

"On my farm, that old hill used to be covered up with them," Lloyd Odum, eighty-three, says. "Big old trees. Three, four, or five men couldn't reach around them. Lord yes, we'd carry the chestnuts to the house, and feed them to the hogs."

Chestnuts for roasting were harvested and shipped by the boxcar-load to eastern cities each autumn, a highly popular street snack. But for rural folk, the tree was indispensable. It was a sturdy prop under a sometimes shaky economy. Rot- and insect-resistant, hard, light, straight-grained, abundant chestnut wood was often the lumber of choice for cabins, barns, shingles, and fence rails, firewood, cribs, coffins, mine timbers, and furniture. "The farmers' hogs were fattened on chestnuts, and to no small degree, his children were also," one historian has written.

Although a hundred different hardwood tree species were used for lumber in the southern Appalachians, chestnut made up more than a quarter of the cut. It also supplied much of the extract for tanning heavy leathers, a major industry.

Its virtual disappearance from 200 million acres of eastern

forest was also a convulsive change for the ecosystem. That preblight chestnut forest was magnificently adapted to its environment, growing at elevations from one thousand to five thousand feet. Up to a hundred feet tall, commonly five or more feet in diameter, the tree was a hardy survivor of steep slopes, poor soils, and drought. A few lived for as long as six centuries.

Though our knowledge is sparse, by any reckoning the chestnut was a keystone species. In the survival game of competing for sunlight in wild forests, chestnut "tends to just explode out of the ground," Purdue researcher Douglass Jacobs says. His studies have found that chestnuts dominate black walnut and red oak, for example, growing more than half again as tall and more than twice as wide during their first eight years.

Turkey, bears, squirrels, jays, and many other animals feed on chestnuts, a much heavier and more reliable annual food crop than acorns. A small hint of that former richness surfaced when scientists attempted to reintroduce red wolves in the southern Appalachians a few years ago. One reason the project failed was that the wolves found too few small mammals to eat. That food chain may well have been depleted when the annual supply of countless billions of chestnuts vanished.

By the 1930s the blight had begun its destructive work around Meadowview. When Odum left the marines after World War II, he got a job dynamiting the stumps of some of the last trees to succumb. "People didn't seem to talk about it much," he recalls. "They just took for granted, you know, that the trees would come back. But they never would."

You can still find chestnut trees scattered through the woods of Maryland and Virginia today, especially in the mountains. They sprout from the half-buried stumps of giants that died seven decades or more ago. A few survive until they're mature enough to bear the tough, spiny burs, about the size of billiard balls, that crack open in the fall to release three glossy chestnuts. But they seldom grow even ten feet tall before the blight invades, bursts open their bark, and kills them. "Fred and them's doing a pretty good job," Odum allows. "Get them trees so they can put them back into the mountains."

The effort to revive the American chestnut has determined much of Hebard's life, and his family's, since 1970. That year, at twenty-two, he found himself working as a farmhand somewhere in Connecticut. "The farmer and I were trailing a heifer that had busted out and gone a long ways," Hebard recalls. "He showed me a chestnut sprout, and just started telling me about it. I thought, well, it would be nice to go back to college and study biology and try to cure chestnut blight. . . . I didn't realize it was a lifetime proposition, back then."

That was enough to keep him in school at Columbia, Michigan, and Virginia Tech. In 1989 he was hired by the nonprofit American Chestnut Foundation to start its breeding and restoration program on a small leased farm. Now there are four staffers, and row on row of thousands of chestnut trees of varying ages and pedigrees, and two more small farms in the same neighborhood.

On one of the farms is that decrepit truck, now being reconfigured with a welding torch. And next to that, several hundred four-foot-tall seedlings blanket a hillside. They are the latest mile markers along Hebard's experimental path. The goal is to capture the blight resistance that's found in the comparatively squat Chinese chestnut tree species and to incorporate it into the DNA of the American tree.

This is to be accomplished with a tree breeder's genetic sleight-of-hand. First, a Chinese and an American tree are crossed. A few of their progeny will inherit the two or three genes that confer blight resistance—a kind of genetic lottery ticket. The winners still have much of the appearance of the Chinese parents, so they are mated with American trees, and that generation is also tested to see which trees carry the resistance genes. The breeding process continues until the Chinese resistance has been transferred to a tree whose genes and structure are almost completely American.

Chestnut trees mature slowly, though, and have to be three or four years old before they can be tested for blight resistance. This means that the research can run to decades, over several generations of trees. Hebard's sets of genetic links have been assembled one day at a time for the last fifteen years, and the work continues. In the meantime, it's all about hailstorms and drought, plowing and planting, spraying against the bugs and weeds, mending the fences, the irrigation, and the broken tractors.

The seedlings on the hillside are the latest-and-greatest generation. In three or four years, the nuts from the ones that have inherited the blight resistance genes will be planted—but not on the farms. For the first time in the project's history, those nuts, 15/16ths American, will be planted out in the wild, perhaps in the nearby Jefferson National Forest.

Then we'll see. The longer they survive, and the more they look like American chestnut trees as they mature, the better. Meanwhile, trees of even greater genetic refinement will continue to be bred back on the farms.

Chestnut sex is pretty easy for humans to master. There's some sweat, and it's a good time—even if you do have to climb up a stepladder. That's lucky, because the success of the Meadowview project also depends on volunteers in a network of state chapters along the chestnut tree's former range, including a thriving chapter in Maryland.

"We have lots of fun doing it," Germantown member Barbara Knapp says. "The whole story of the chestnut is addictive. Getting this magnificent tree back into the Appalachians, even if I'll never see it . . . it's a very exciting prospect."

Knapp is one of several dozen Maryland volunteers who plant and pollinate among native chestnut groves—terminally blighted but, for now, reproducing—at the base of Sugarloaf Mountain and near Thurmont. They are trying to make sure the regional genetic variations that have allowed chestnuts to adapt to the soils and climate of Maryland, Maine, or Georgia are not lost as the blight resistance breeding project ramps up.

The first thing to know is that chestnut trees are bisexual.

In late spring, each bears starbursts of long, fuzzy, cream-colored male catkins. Each tree also has dozens of small, green female flowers, but a tree cannot pollinate itself. And not just any pollen is welcome. Hebard is exporting pollen from his hybrid trees to volunteer matchmakers all over the East. Then the volunteers pollinate local, specially chosen "mother trees" that have escaped the blight long enough to reproduce. (The Massachusetts chapter calls its campaign "the American chestnut dating service.") At least some of the resulting crop of nuts will carry both the blight resistance genes and the localized survival traits. To get all this done, these far-flung volunteers emulate the human-assisted mating dance that occurs at the Meadowview Farms. There, Hebard, his staff, and groups of volunteers all put in hundreds of hours atop ladders or cherry-picker cranes.

Each chestnut tree that has reached reproductive age is spreading pollen in the breezes and also presenting receptive female flowers to all comers. If you're trying to control that unruly, indiscriminate mating process to narrow the genetics of their offspring, you have to take extraordinary measures.

About mid-June, "we put special bags very tightly over the female flowers so that any wandering pollen can't get in, and pull off the male catkins that are near these particular flowers," Knapp says. "And then about ten days later we get pollen from the nursery down in Virginia, and we open up the bags and brush the pollen onto the female flowers." Then the bags are put back in place, and the resulting chestnuts are of known parentage.

But perhaps the most demanding work, especially for retirees who come to Meadowview to help, is testing young trees to see whether they are blight resistant. This is stoop labor, performed by pushing your way through a faceful of stiff branches to the base of the tree, augering a hole in the trunk, then administering dollops of two different strains of chestnut blight. Their survival rate is one measure of the success of the whole long project.

Sandra Anagnostakis is a longtime chestnut research scientist in Connecticut who collaborates with Hebard on some of the tree-breeding work. She breaks into laughter when asked if there are any nonbelievers. "Most people just think it's too much work. It all depends on whether you put in the time and effort. The problem is, does anyone have the faith and the money and the time to do it? Of course it'll work. These are just simple breeding principles."

Just the same, failure is a possibility. With time, the blight might adapt to the "new" tree's defenses and overcome them. The Chinese genetic component, though proportionally small, might still be enough to strongly influence the tree's structure and appearance as it matures. The resistance could start strong and then break down. Some unknown factor might prevent the newly invented tree's ability to survive out in the woods.

Hebard is not reluctant to point out these shadows. And a pessimist might call to mind the daunting history of attempts to resuscitate the chestnut forest, including earlier breeding experiments and searches for resistant trees. There were acid sprays, poisons, poultices, quarantines, grafts, treatments with sulfur fumes and rusty nails, nuclear irradiation, and a fungus that was supposed to kill the chestnut blight but not the tree. Just a few have proved worthy of further tinkering.

Naturally, Hebard gives the Meadowview project very good odds of success, but he has plenty of company. Indeed, its breeding program was first worked out and proposed by an eminent plant geneticist, the late Charles Burnham. The soundness of the approach has since been reviewed and confirmed by two independent science panels.

Votes of confidence have also been registered recently by the feds. Jim Sherald, regional chief of natural resources and science for the National Park Service, calls Meadowview "not doubtful, but hopeful. . . . It's certainly the avenue that holds the most promise for now." Plans for reintroducing the hoped-for, blight-free chestnut tree to southeastern national parks in the future are already under discussion. Even more significantly, cash support from the U.S. Forest Service spiked to $250,000 this year, boosting the American Chestnut Foundation's budget by about 25 percent.

Elsewhere, biotechnicians are also attempting to revive the chestnut with gene sequencing machines and microscopic tweezers. They hope someday to splice blight-resistant genes into chestnut trees and make a high-tech end run around most of the tedious tree breeding. They salute the Meadowview project as important work, however.

Even if some laboratory breakthrough were on the far horizon, it would still have to be proved out in the field, patiently, sometimes beyond the life spans of the researchers. "Ninety-five percent of all tree-breeding efforts are still like what our ancestors did thousands of years ago, only more refined," says Rob Mangold, a geneticist who directs the Forest Service's Forest Health Protection program.

Hebard, too, has done time over a microscope. But he decided early on that he probably works best out on the land. A half-hour drive south from Meadowview takes you along a steepening, overgrown old logging track, up into the Jefferson National Forest along Chestnut Ridge, which in turn is part of Iron Mountain. At perhaps the 3,000-foot elevation, Hebard has negotiated his truck to where the road is impassable—acquiescing, finally, to the incline, and the dense tangle of forest.

That journey links the carefully groomed rank and file of hybrid trees down on the Meadowview chestnut research farms with the wild, native side of their genetics. We're looking at a desolate grove of shrubby American chestnuts—all terminal cases, their trunks already burst open by the blight. They have resprouted from the stumps of the huge trees that used to shade this part of the mountain long ago.

The thought of reclaiming that immense, vanished forest is deeply agreeable. But it will take far longer to restore than consigning it to biological oblivion did. It will take patient labor, distant goals, to suit the slower rhythms of the lives of trees. "If there's any genius in what I'm doing here, it's just growing these trees out to an age where they can be tested and survive," Hebard says. "Biting the bullet, and planting out the acreages."

And of course, the real success of the Meadowview project will only be guaranteed after he's in the ground himself—when those experimental American chestnuts to be planted out in the wild are fifty or a hundred years old and look like, and thrive as certainly as, their lost ancestors.

Small Books,
Old Stories

In an office lab in West Philadelphia, Naomi Miller sits transfixed, peering down through the twin barrels of a microscope. Around her is a sort of sarcophagus for long-dead plants and seeds, in phials and film canisters or mounted for reference.

There are no exotic trophies or travel posters—just a death row of potted plants on the window sill, so neglected that they look ready to join the specimens in the steel cabinets. She pushes burnt seeds and splinters in and out of the field of view with a slender paintbrush, identifying and counting by species. She once told an acquaintance, half in jest, that the only reason she got into this line of work was that it was so boring no one else would touch it.

Out from behind the microscope, however, Miller's vision is as panoramic as the vivid Near Eastern watercolor landscapes she has painted over the course of her career. For her research has given us, among other things, a clearer picture of the domestication of animals and plants over long reaches of time, and of the resulting transformation of human history and culture. Some of the implications of what she has turned up extend even further, into our own future.

A lanky fifty-three-year-old with a guileless look that shouldn't be mistaken for naivete, Miller is a senior research scientist at the University of Pennsylvania's Museum Applied Science Center for Archaeology. Her specialty is paleoethnobotany, aka archaeobotany, which studies the surviving traces of plant materials used by humans in ancient times—seeds, charcoal, fiber, wood, pollen, and plant-generated silica. For some thirty years she has poked through and peered at what humans and livestock ate and drank, what plant materials were used for clothes, tools, or construction, how agriculture altered human culture and how humans reshaped, and have at times despoiled, their natural environment and their own prospects for survival.

Archaeobotany was a relatively new field when Miller began her career in the late 1970s. At the time, most of the small number of practicing archaeobotanists chose to remain in their labs rather than participating in excavations at archaeological sites. A few worked at digs in North America, but that was "home," where you didn't have to learn a language, exist by yourself in a village, and manage both plant collecting and archaeological analysis. "At least in the Middle East, Naomi was pretty unique," veteran archaeologist Mary Voigt of the College of William and Mary says.

So Miller went to southwestern Iran, to the site of the ancient Elamite city of Anshan (now Malyan). Her work there, analyzing plant remains from a five-thousand-year-old urban setting, was interrupted by the Iranian revolution, which banished a generation of foreign archaeologists from the country. She left with her seed collection—like a precious library of ancient stories to be decoded from tiny books—in her luggage in 1978, and with little hope of returning.

Iran was once again on the agenda, however, during a recent morning at Miller's spartan Philadelphia headquarters—part of a basement-level warren of splintered doorframes, concrete floors, and boarded-up windows (the building is in the noisy throes of what looks to be a much-needed renovation). She is weighing fresh invitations to return to Iran for work at Susiana, another Elamite-era dig. Miller has the energy of a grad student, her colleagues say, oddly combined with a lot of forbearance. The life of your average Near Eastern archaeologist can be trying: spending hours at a gritty, sweltering excavation, only to find that nobody's been screening or sampling. Back at the lab, the mice have eaten all the labels. A shower might redeem some of this, but no one's bothered to fire up the hot-water heater. And the household has run out of vodka. So patience among colleagues can stretch thin, but Miller is rarely if ever dispirited or moody, those who have worked with her say. By all accounts she is an optimist—a sustaining presence when the conditions of archaeological life wear on the spirit. She bakes desserts, sings the "Marseillaise" on Bastille Day, and plays the kazoo at birthdays. And then there are her drawings and illustrations. "Naomi's art work has always been a humorous commentary on the life at archaeological digs, and that helps relieve pressure," says Smithsonian archaeologist Melinda Zeder. "It's a way of capturing our unusual life situations, and the reactions of natives to us."

The wry humor has been known to give way, just the same. It was a once-in-a-decade sort of thing, but Miller once confronted a Turkish official—the breed of Eminence that foreign archaeologists are obliged to defer to—after he had prevented a carload of her hot and exhausted co-workers from departing. They waited while he extended an already languorous meal of fish. After telling him off at length in his own language and well within earshot of the other restaurant patrons, Miller strode to the car, yanked out his luggage, and heaved it into the road.

Indeed, Miller speaks Turkish well and has excellent French. She speaks and reads German and Russian and can handle Dutch and ancient Sumerian. She also loves to talk.

"She will talk to anybody about anything," says Voigt. "She's unusual even among archaeologists, and we are a lot of talkers. I spent a week in Iran with her. At first, her Persian was pretty weak. But she just kept working on it, engaging everybody in conversations. It was amazing."

That tendency to mingle informed Miller's research at Anshan. She was curious about the lives of both the ancient and the contemporary citizenry, and fortunately, as things turned out, was ready to engage them both.

Archaeobotany begins with the low-tech tedium of flotation—dumping soil samples into vats of water, to separate and sieve out the materials of interest. (Among the verities: bone sinks; seeds and charcoal float; plant remains are almost never preserved in dirt unless they're charred.) Flotation gleanings are examined under a low-power microscope and manually sorted and counted by species—maybe juniper or pistachio wood, wheat, trigonella, or camelthorn seeds. One fleck at a time.

In Anshan, Miller was soon charting the shifting ratios of charcoal and seeds, as registered in strata deposited over thousands of years. Burnt seeds show up among the hearth ashes at many Near East excavations. At the time, they were interpreted only as the remains of spilled food, though it seemed odd to Miller how often spills seemed to occur.

The Anshan finds were even more puzzling: a preponderance of wild, nonfood plant seeds in a place where wheat and barley had been cultivated for thousands of years. Other questions emerged from the ashes: Why was the proportion of charcoal to charred seeds greater in 3000 BC than in 2000 BC, indicating a shift away from the use of wood as cooking fuel, as the centuries passed?

Following a hunch, Miller visited a nearby village to see how the locals lived. After all, what did a Michigan grad student raised in the Bronx know about rural life in a Near Eastern landscape? "I began to observe how plants were incorporated into what would become the archaeological record," she recalls. "How they got charred and disposed of, in a community without electricity, running water, or gas lines."

She soon learned that local cooking fires differed little from those of Elamite times. Animal dung was still used, and Miller began to wonder whether it might contain seeds. She discreetly scooped up some hearth sweepings to ship home. Lab analy-

sis made it apparent that archaeologists had often been looking at the seeds in the remains of animal diets, in the form of
burned dung, rather than seeds from spilled human food. That
explained the presence of so many wild plant seeds in ancient
hearths. It also suggested a reason for the increasing ratio of
seeds to charcoal over time: as Anshan's population increased,
wood became scarcer and more remote. Nearby forests were re-
lentlessly cleared for fuel and construction, and to open fields
for agriculture. People began to burn dung instead.

Miller's findings are now widely accepted as applicable to
many other Near East sites. Her career-long investigations in
Turkey, Turkmenistan, Syria, and Israel have yielded a steady
stream of technical research papers about the tally of plant
materials at different settlements. Moreover, those prosaic bits
of charred wood and seeds have raised some basic questions
about whole landscapes and the cultures they sustain. Ohio
State University archaeologist Joy McCorriston says Miller has
been "connecting the dots, and making important contributions where she pulls it all together."

Miller's work has helped archaeobotanists to link their data
into a sort of house-that-Jack-built story line. The ratios of
plant remains reflect the impact of population growth, agriculture, and local industry on the environment. They record how
pasture quality deteriorates under grazing pressure, and how
forests vanish permanently, transformed into timber and fu-
elwood. The depth of valley erosion sediments illustrates how
quickly denuded hills can lose their productive soils. And that
explains why, in many places, the trees did not return.

Degraded pastures and deforestation mean less food and
fuel, altering the conditions of life and survival options for the
inhabitants. At some point, unsustainable cultures are forced
into population decline, or abandonment.

Climate shifts—catastrophic drought and flooding—have
often been put forward by archaeologists as the prime mover
in the abrupt demise of many early cultural centers. Miller's
work suggests a different emphasis, says Mary Voigt. It is "put-

ting people back into issues of environmental change, where they should be and where, increasingly, we think of them today. We have not thought that way about the deep past. She is a leader in shifting the emphasis from climate to people."

Perhaps the most prominent of her scholarly dust-ups so far occurred when Miller wrote an article questioning the results of a survey of botanical evidence at the Abu Hureyra site in what is now northern Syria, which involved decades of research by the British archaeobotanist Gordon Hillman. His team had interpreted the mixes of several species of seed concentrations as evidence that humans harvested a variety of wild plants—a kind of prelude to agriculture.

Miller suggested those seed concentrations might be burnt gazelle dung instead. Gazelle were fairly common at the time, and a known source of meat. Detailed counterpoints from both sides ensued.

Over time, in each of these conflicts, the accumulation of evidence will tilt the scales toward or away from Miller's conclusions—or someone will suggest a new idea. As for the provenance of the seeds at Abu Hureyra, Miller says, "I still think it's gazelle shit."

Miller has written, "Human populations carry out their daily lives within a natural environment that has its own, sometimes unforgiving, qualities, and land use practices that favor short-term economic advantage over long-term, sustainable resource management may adversely affect later generations." She's more than a little uneasy about how our own civilization is doing on that score.

"History demonstrates," she says with a self-mocking laugh at the grandiosity of the observation, "that the chances of something positive happening are actually pretty slender." She says people should think long-term—like archaeologists— when they introduce ecological change.

"I don't think we should all become hunter-gatherers again. I accept modern industrial society, and I also think that everything changes—nothing's going to stay the same. The trick is to slow down change, so if you do start seeing change you can actually have time to make the adjustment. It's much easier to maintain the ecosystem than it is to repair it. The problem is that most people in policy-making positions don't care.

"The social value of archaeology," she says, "is putting people in their place—giving them a sense that we are one little part of a very long continuum. It includes not just other humans. Things have happened before us and will happen after us. Basically, the social function of archaeology is to teach humility—and that we should pay attention."

Last Stand

Jesse Overcash holds an old aerial photo up to the light—a few square miles of southwestern Virginia mountains, circa 1935. His finger traces an upfold in the blanket of forest, near a place called Griffith Knob.

"You can look at the different textures here, and the density of those crowns of trees—they're part of a continuum," he says. The rarest part of it, in fact. A darker stretch near the bottom of the image suggests the canopies of big, and very old, trees.

Of course, that whole section may have been clear-cut for saw timber or wood pulp during the intervening decades. Overcash has weighed the possibilities. The annals of the Jefferson National Forest, which go back seventy years or so, show no logging just there. On the other hand, records were sketchy back then. He runs a fingernail over the steep contour lines on a topographic map of the area. The terrain would have been tough for loggers to get to.

So some fairly intense bushwhacking is in order, to go take a look. This might turn out to be the kind of discovery Overcash has occasionally gleaned from several years of detective work. It could be one of eastern America's exceedingly rare un-logged—aka primary, virgin, original, or old-growth—forests.

A career biologist at the Blacksburg outpost of the U.S. Forest Service, Overcash has a professional interest in these relic forests, whittled over the last couple of centuries to wisps of habitat for a rich variety of wildlife. He knows their value to science, and to the lumber mill.

In the khaki uniform of federal forestry, with a country-western twang and a taste for fresh venison, Overcash is no stereotypical tree hugger. But he is not immune to the mystery and melancholy of the lost forests of the mid-Atlantic, where trees were ten stories tall and as wide as two men lying head to toe. "The first thing is, I just like big trees," says Overcash. "If I could come back, I would like to come back when there were forests of them. Imagine seeing a twelve-foot-diameter white oak!"

Bigger, even. Just across the Potomac from Maryland, on a day in 1913, loggers axe-notched three sides of a huge white oak, then felled it with a two-man cross-cut saw, during what must have been an epic labor. The giant at Lead Mine, West Virginia, measured thirteen feet through its base.

Get up for a minute and pace it off on the carpet, if the room you're in happens to be large enough. Imagine a tree trunk to fit that dimension, rising 120 feet into the sky. Then picture legions of other trees nearly as large: several thousand square miles of poplars, sugar maples and sycamores, spruce and fir, black, red, and scarlet oaks, chestnuts, basswoods, beech, black cherries.

Perform that bit of time travel and you've touched the dim outlines of the vast green ocean of original mid-Appalachian forests, before they were cut, acre by acre, county by county, until they were all but gone.

Dwindling reserves of never-logged forest have been the ground of savage political conflicts for the past thirty years in the Pacific Northwest. In that region, only some 5 percent of the original forest remains. But until recently, the scattered examples of old growth that are turning up in the Atlantic states weren't believed to exist at all. They nearly do not. Remaining old growth may constitute as little as half of 1 percent of the vast eastern ur-forests that stunned the first European settlers.

Scientists and self-schooled naturalists have been scouting out patches of old growth since the mid-1990s, and gradually the official stewards of public lands have become more interested in the search. Ecological detective work similar to Overcash's is under way in Maryland, where the state Department of Natural Resources is conducting a survey of old growth.

If the recent past is any guide, new entries in this slender catalog of remnants could be of great value to science. They will certainly become part of the debate over whether commercial uses—roading, logging, mining, and drilling on national and state forests—should be accelerated, or halted altogether.

When Overcash's career with the Forest Service began in the 1980s, there was little official reverence for old growth, often referred to as "decadent"—past its prime as marketable timber and overdue for harvest. Two events nudged him out of the mainstream. The first was the agency's approval of a logging operation in an old grove.

"I tell you what," he recalls. "We cut a stand here just because we could, back in '89; that irritated me to death. It was some beautiful white oak. I said, let's don't cut this, and we did anyway. And from that day on, it was—all right, I'm not going to relent on this issue."

Around that time, Overcash came across those Depression-era aerial photos of national forest lands, taken just after they were acquired by the government. Since then, he has mined them for clues about where to find old-growth, or "original," forests that are often hidden among hundreds of thousands of acres of comparatively skinny, brushy, younger forest in the rugged Appalachian uplands.

"Everybody here knows pretty much what I'm about, and they've taken well to it over time," Overcash says. "It's been interesting. In a land management agency, being a forceful advocate for old growth has not always been the most popular thing to do. There are definitely people who couldn't care less, because to them it is just wood."

Old-growth forests are also repositories of what we know, or can yet discover, about how forest ecosystems evolve when they're out from under the hand of humankind, but preserving them is no easy thing. Through a combination of perseverance and passion, Overcash and a handful of others have at least been able to make the significance of old-growth forests more visible.

Madison's Mind-Set

"I'm a dendrochronologist. We have a vested interest in old trees," David Stahle of the University of Arkansas will tell you. "There are interesting plants and animals here in a kind of uncorrupted ecosystem that tells a lot about our heavy footprint on the land."

Under a microscope, tree rings are ledgers, whose occasional charred pages can tell him the frequency of fire in earlier centuries. They have clarified disputes over how extensively Indians burned the woods, or for that matter, how often they require burning, in order for certain kinds of oak and pine to reproduce.

Some research suggests that our success in suppressing forest fires is causing the disappearance of oaks up and down the Appalachian chain. "There is massive change in the understory of oak forest," says Penn State forest ecologist Marc Abrams, who has studied the role of fire in Maryland and Virginia old growth. "It looks like oak forests are now going to be dominated by red maple, sugar maple, birch, beech, and cherry."

Old forests also serve as important proxy measures of climate change. "There's no other annual record of environmental change sitting out on the natural landscape for three hundred to five hundred years, than trees," says Ed Cook of Columbia University. "Nothing else like it in the natural world." Cook's research team is studying Eastern red cedars on remote cliff faces in the Virginias. They have discovered segments of long-dead cedar trunks that push the climate chronology back to the year 481 AD, and there is hope of going further.

According to the trees, it's getting hotter. "High-elevation and high-latitude tree-ring chronologies tell us quite clearly that the twentieth century has been unusual over the last thousand years," Stahle says. "Natural forces we are aware of cannot explain the warming. There is an incredible surge in tree growth."

Old trees are rare, but they're around, even in the Washington, D.C., area. There are small pockets at Turkey Run along the George Washington Parkway, at Great Falls Park, at Arlington National Cemetery. Some chestnut oaks that Stahle has a hunch may be six hundred years old are a short walk from the Blue Ridge Parkway.

But intact old-forest ecosystems—the whole web of soils, streams, and living organisms—tell a much more complex story than individual old trees. "It's not just tree rings. It's the whole package," Stahle says. "We humans have intervened ecologically and now we are trying to figure out: how do these systems function naturally?"

One fragile vestige of an old-growth ecosystem is two hundred acres of forest at Montpelier, the estate of President James Madison in Orange County, Virginia. This is prime farmland, laid out in the 1720s along the same low ridge as Jefferson's Monticello, thirty miles to the south.

"We don't really know why this section wasn't completely cut," says Dan Druckenbrod, a doctoral candidate in ecology at the University of Virginia. "But President Madison did have a kind of sympathy for the loss of forests."

It might be a stretch to call him an agitator for old-growth preservation, but in a speech to the Agricultural Society of Albemarle County in 1818, Madison, by then in his late sixties, told the local farmers that he was vexed by "the injudicious and excessive destruction of timber and firewood."

The same sensibility mixed, perhaps, with benign neglect, has protected Montpelier's old growth through a long chain of ownerships. The oldest tree Druckenbrod has found so far, the battered ghost of a white oak that sentinels its little ravine, dates back to 1712—that's twenty years before George Washington was born.

Some researchers apologize for eastern old growth a bit, con-

cerned lest a visitor feel disappointment at the lack of giant se-
quoias, or of fairy-tale spookvoodoo. But the massive, limbless
straight trunks of the poplars, oaks, hickories, and ash trees at
Montpelier can easily startle. A few are four feet in diameter,
and the farthest reaches of high canopy soar out a hundred
feet or more above, nearly lost to sight.

In midday these vaulted spaces are mostly still, dappled
shade. Only the occasional songs of wood thrush and the
mighty thocks of a pileated woodpecker part the silence. Here
and there, the stumps and husks of long-dead chestnut trees,
once prized for their stubborn resistance to insects and decay,
quietly turn to dust.

But there is abundant evidence that this is not a museum.
The scene is one of violent action, albeit in slow motion. Imagine a couple of centuries of forest history in fast-forward, and
trees thrust up from the hillside like giant fists. Waves of fire,
lightning, gale winds, and insect infestation roll through.
Blown-over trees lever up Medusa-heads of clods and roots ten
feet across and leave gaping craters, a pattern that ecologists
call "pit and mound topography."

The constant tumult allows light to pour through gaps in
the canopy, stimulating new growth on the forest floor. That
creates a mix of old, young, and dead trees. It also opens niches
that offer feeding and breeding prospects for a wide range of
species that have evolved to make use of them. Bears like to
den in the hollows of big old trees, for example.

Unlogged forests also support a wider diversity of less common kinds of plants. Research at the University of Georgia
paired nine Appalachian old-growth sites with others that had
been clear-cut as long as eighty-seven years before. Even after
this much time had passed, the number of different species of
plants on the logged sites was severely reduced, and was not
recovering. "If anything, both richness and cover appeared to
be decreasing," the study found.

But to think of Montpelier or any other forest as pristine,
while it may fire the imagination, is a mistake. "It denies the

human impact on the land," Druckenbrod reminds. Even without logging or roading, any eastern forest has been altered by acid rain, ozone pollution, climate change, and a long list of introduced species such as gypsy moth and kudzu. The Indians burned forests to an unknown extent. The Asian chestnut blight early last century erased a key component of the ecosystem, and in many otherwise untouched forests, the dying chestnuts were salvaged by loggers.

So no forest is absolutely "natural." Instead, the possibilities run from tame to near-wild. Tree farms—biologically simplified, same-age-same-species-same-genes, like a big lawn—are at one end of that scale. At the other end are the diverse, complex, old-growth landscapes in which—even if traces of human influence are present—natural forces have always predominated.

What's Enough

In one such place—a parklike grove of mountain old growth in Maryland—the curious buzz-notes of a cerulean warbler tickle the air. About the size of a finch, the bird, a male, flicks down to a lower limb to show a black collar and striking, silver-blue head- and wing-feathers.

On the few occasions when scientists can decipher them, living organisms like this one are bioindicators, a kind of living recapitulation of environmental conditions. Over the summer, ceruleans—they are denizens of large expanses of mature forest—were reported as largely missing from several of their usual nesting spots up and down the Appalachians.

One season means little, but according to an annual federal survey, this species' numbers plummeted more than 77 percent from 1966 to 2004. That's probably one of the fastest vanishing acts among many kinds of migratory songbirds in trouble in the East. The Audubon Society and twenty-seven other environmental groups have threatened to file suit to force the United States to designate the once-common cerulean as a threatened species.

"When a species like the cerulean warbler, which occurs over a fairly large area, is disappearing at this rate, clearly something big is happening," says Jeffrey Wells of the Audubon's science office. One unanswered question: where are the most significant changes in its bicontinental habitat occurring? The cerulean winters at midelevations along the Andes from Venezuela to Peru and then, in a display of endurance almost beyond imagining, migrates several thousand miles each spring to nest in large expanses of mature forests in the eastern United States. Another mystery is just how large a protected forest is required for this—and the other interior forest species that are in trouble—to maintain their populations.

It's not an uncommon story line these days. As conservation biologists have monitored the survival trajectories of one declining species after another over the past generation, the caseload has merged into a larger picture. Biological diversity wanes, and the need for more and larger forests, off-limits to logging and roading, presses.

The comparison may jar, but this predicament echoes what we face with nuclear waste dumps. Because of the power we now wield over nature, we are called upon to try to anticipate, as never before, circumstances far in the future. Out at Yucca Mountain, Nevada, or wherever we decide to leave the stuff, we are trying to design a crypt for our nuclear poisons so carefully wrought that it will keep humans from harm for thousands of years.

For the mountain ecosystems of Virginia and Maryland, conservation biologists must puzzle out their plans with an eye on the same near-cosmic calendar, hundreds and thousands of years long. They are trying to think through all the circumstances that could head wild species away from, rather than toward, extinction. To do that, you protect not just individual species, but the intact ecosystems that sustain them. So if the great game is the long-term survival chances of whole ecosystems, you need an Ark—a large fleet of them, really—to bear the whole biological assemblage on into the indefinite future.

The Book of Genesis relates that Noah didn't have to figure out how big the Ark should be. He was given the blueprints. In the absence of that kind of guidance, conservation biologists are trying to do the figuring. How big do our vessels—protected forests—have to be, for ecosystems to survive?

The "how much is enough for wildlife?" question is relatively new. Our state and national forests have been managed since their inception under a different idea called "multiple use." That is: parcel them out to hikers, hang-gliders, hunters, ATV owners, miners, drillers, and, of course, loggers. Some of these groups have more political voltage at their disposal than others, and over time, that determines how the forests are gerrymandered among the claimants. That helps explain why in Virginia's Jefferson National Forest there are three thousand miles of roads and two thousand miles of hiking trails, and why slightly more than half of Maryland's state forests are open to some form of logging.

Thinking of publicly owned forests as the last refuges for wild species makes multiple-use proponents, especially those with economic interests at stake, deeply suspicious. They have been asked to yield acreage for hitherto obscure salamanders, birds, rare plants, old trees. If a thousand acres are on the table, their argument goes, why not just be fair and split the difference?

Conservation biologists have come to see a different landscape. They say the "multiple-use" mentality ignores history: natural areas have already been pieced off, over and over again, for four hundred years. In that process, each fair-looking fifty-fifty bargain has left a tinier splinter of the original habitat and a longer list of species in peril. Public lands are all that's left.

An instructive case survives, more or less, at Belt Woods, a Prince Georges County, Maryland, preserve of forty-three acres of magnificent oaks, maples, and poplars, some of them four hundred years old, within a somewhat larger and younger forest. Protected from real estate development after an epic battle a few years back, Belt Woods displays both the biological richness of old-growth forests and the vulnerability of the smaller ones.

"Look at this example, and you see what's happened," says wildlife biologist Chandler Robbins, who began studying birds there in 1947. "When we initially worked in Belt Woods, we found there were extraordinarily high nesting bird populations," he says. But they are dropping off in recent years. This small forest island in an encroaching suburban sea affords too little protection from outside influences. High winds mauled one section. Overabundant deer are browsing away the understory plants. And the smaller the forest, the higher its ratio of edge, compared to total area. That means it is prone to invasions of edge-dwelling predators—snakes, possums, raccoons, domestic cats—and a ubiquitous nest parasite, the cowbird.

"The larger your area is and the more protected it is, the more species you are going to end up with," Robbins says, summarizing dozens of research studies of fragmented habitat. "We need to plan for an increasing number of contiguous, maturing forests."

The same shadow falls across the future of the forty acres of old hemlocks at Swallow Falls State Park in Maryland, and the only old growth in all of Virginia's fifty-thousand-acre state forest system—a mere forty acres at Turkey Ridge, an hour's drive east of Richmond.

The portfolio of the nonprofit Nature Conservancy, which often buys private land in order to protect it, includes an old-growth enclave at Cranesville Swamp, Maryland. "As an ecologist I like them, I appreciate them," says state Conservancy science director Douglas Samson. But he doubts that such places can retain their biological character unless they are buffered by large, protected, surrounding forests. "Two thousand acres begins to function as a mature forest," Samson says. "Cranesville is a few acres."

So how big does a forest need to be to absorb the natural "disturbance regime"—the unavoidable and ecologically necessary hurricanes, insect outbreaks, ice storms, and fires—and protect a full suite of plant and animal species, so some other generation can decide its fate?

In the mountains of Maryland and Virginia, the Conservancy's national science staff has concluded that ideal forest would be something like ten thousand to fifteen thousand acres at least. Few if any of those are on the market, of course, but the general idea remains: the bigger the protected forest the better, and as many as possible, please.

"The hope is that we can find places that will take on the character of wilderness forest, undisturbed except by natural forces," Samson says. Those places are the paradoxically named "future old growth." Depending on the type and condition of the forest, the process of restoring their wilderness character could take several centuries.

"How much is enough?" is about scale. And in this controversy, numbers that look solid at first glance can quickly turn rubbery, as both sides add and subtract to make their case. Take some outer-limits numbers, just for discussion. Let's say you turn all Maryland's state forests into wildlands, which enjoy the stoutest protection. You would have set aside less than 2 percent of the state's land base—and perhaps 5 percent of all of the forested land in the state, public and private—as "future old growth." Is that too much, or not enough? Officially designated wildlands currently total about seven one-thousandths of Maryland's land base. Too much, or not enough?

Federal "wilderness" is the equivalent of Maryland's state-owned wildlands. In the unlikely event that all Virginia's federal national forest lands were protected as wilderness, less than 9 percent of the state, and 15 percent of current forested lands, both public and private, would very gradually return to a semblance of the original pre-European forest. Today, officially designated wilderness areas occupy about six one-thousandths of Virginia.

One Big Park

Current arrangements deal with the environment pretty generously, in the eyes of Maryland Del. George C. Edwards, Republican, who represents Garrett and Allegany counties, which account for a lopsided 85 percent or so of the acreage of the state forest system, depending on how you tally. After resisting the campaigns of environmentalists for years, Edwards agreed to sponsor legislation in recent years that designated 4,400 acres of state forest along the Savage River—much of it old growth—as wildlands. But his understanding is, that's about the last of it.

"The heritage of this county is timbering and mineral extraction and those kinds of things," he says. "Over the years you have the state coming in and buying up all kinds of land, just because it is the cheapest place they could buy it, and then doing things to discourage people from mining or timber harvesting."

Resource-extraction jobs help the local economy in this, chronically one of the poorer parts of the state, but the economic value of logging is disputed. Some state forest logging revenues are returned to counties to offset the impact of public land on local tax rolls. It amounts to some 1 percent of Garrett County's revenues; half of 1 percent in Allegany County.

"And the feeling here is," Edwards says, "a lot of people down East would just like to put a big gate up around it and say we have one big park and that's it."

What about letting it all mature into future old growth, the best simulation of virgin forest we can manage? "These people who yell about cutting trees up here, what are they doing to stop all the tree-cutting in their woods?" he asks.

This echoes the national debate. The Public Interest Research Group, the Sierra Club, and other environmental groups want to halt logging on all national forests, essentially letting them become future old growth. In 2002, 221 scientists petitioned President Bush with the same demand. They include a half-dozen faculty at campuses in Maryland and Virginia, as well as big-name conservation biologists such as Harvard's Edward O. Wilson and Peter Raven, recipient of the President's National Medal of Science.

"Today almost all of our old growth forests are gone and the timber industry has turned our national forests into a patchwork of clearcuts, logging roads, and devastated habitat," they charge.

Environmentalists and their scientist allies have little influence for now, however. One of George W. Bush's campaign promises was to put public lands "back to work." His appointee in the Interior Department with responsibility for the national forest system is Mark Rey, whose resume includes a long stint as a lobbyist for the American Forest and Paper Association (AFPA). John Mechem, a current AFPA spokesman, details the industry view:

"One of the problems is you've got all these environmentalists saying don't cut old growth, don't cut old growth, yet there's no agreed-upon definition of what old growth is." He's right, if you assume that the discussion shifts as environmentalists hope it will. "Future old growth" can mean any forest where old growth might be restored, in time.

"The environmentalists have made a huge issue of old growth," Mechem continues. "If it is defined too broadly . . . it would essentially be a public relations nightmare for us. If it is defined too broadly, it eliminates a large source of potential harvestable lumber."

Not that it would jolt the timber market much to stop logging on state and national forests. Policies can always change, but just now, public lands supply only a tiny fraction of the national appetite for wood. In Maryland, an average of less than 3 percent of logging is on public land each year, by acreage. National forests account for even less: four-tenths of 1 percent of the U.S. timber harvest.

Maryland DNR biologist Ed Thompson says: "In my mind, the aging second-growth forests are where the real controversy is going to be in coming years. How are we going to manage them?"

Invaders

Burly, bearded Thompson, a natural heritage biologist for the Maryland DNR, clambers easily among ankle-wrenching sandstone outcrops, snag thickets, face-level catbriers, and the hemlocks and sugar maples—some of them four hundred years old—on the south side of Big Savage Mountain, in Garrett County.

These are the ridges tramped by the great old Maryland woodsman Meshach Browning during the first half of the 1800s. His memoir, *Forty-four Years in the Life of a Hunter*, described this as "a country abounding in the finest pine timber, together with oak, curled maple, birch and chestnut timber," and the scattered inhabitants of the valleys as "in the full enjoyment of peace and plenty." He also described a grand profusion of brook trout, bears, wolves, panthers, deer, otters, foxes, turkey, and other game—so much game as to make the forests of the day sound downright congested, though Browning alone killed (and ate) hundreds of them.

Some of those species are entirely missing today. The populations of nearly all are depleted. Only one—the deer—is superabundant. But it is worth celebrating that this, a fair expanse of old forest on Big Savage Mountain, has persisted mostly uncut through a series of near-misses and several years of hard, even desperate, campaigning by old-growth advocates in and out of government service. They are now officially protected state wildlands. It becomes clear during the hike with Thompson, however, that these wildlands will need more than just a ban on logging if they are to survive as relatively unmolested native ecosystems.

"Deer haven't been much of a problem back in here," Thompson says at the edge of the old growth, but he hasn't been through this section in five years. An hour later we stop, where the mountain levels off a little. A fallen oak has opened a light gap in the canopy overhead. On the ground, new young trees, especially oaks, ought to be springing up.

This opening is largely barren, however, because deer have nibbled it clean. "I haven't often seen a little area that has been hammered as hard by deer as this one," Thompson says, fingering a gnawed and leafless stem. It has been the same most of the way, with evidence of browsed foliage even in rocky places that deer usually avoid, and Thompson seems unsettled by the intensity of the deer pressure on regrowth. Without the long-absent cougars and wolves to keep their numbers in check, deer populations are unnaturally high, and growing.

Among the boulders in a sandstone slide, he comes across bouquets of native hay-scented fern, prickly gooseberry, and clearweed, layered like deep-green frosting over the rocks. But there are also pockets of the aggressive Eurasian weed called garlic mustard that were not here before, and they are obviously spreading. It is one of a growing list of invasive alien plants, insects, and diseases that are disrupting native ecosystems.

The old logging road up the mountain showcases at least a half-dozen different Asian and European invasives. "Some places that are very rich may have, say, a hundred species of herbaceous plants," Thompson says. "After you get garlic mustard and Japanese stiltgrass, you come back there in five years and it has maybe thirty or less." Big Savage is, by some temporary good fortune, still free of the hemlock woolly adelgid, an Asian insect that is killing nearly all hemlocks in forests from Connecticut to North Carolina. It has already been spotted in Maryland.

It is cheaper and easier to manage natural areas by stepping back to let nature run the show. But they are already so altered by human influences that the show threatens to unravel without active help. Increasingly, old-growth advocates are arguing that the remaining patches of these ecosystems can be kept intact only by surrounding them with a buffer of protected forests, and by controlling deer populations and invasive species.

Just to the south along Backbone Mountain, within the Potomac-Garrett State Forest, is an old-growth forest that may total several hundred acres, along Crabtree Hollow. Two Ohio University ecologists have described it in a research paper as "the best example of old-growth vegetation remaining in western Maryland."

This is part of a DNR "special management zone," currently off the list of possible logging sites, but without permanent legislative protection. At its entrance during a recent visit there is a locked gate, but a yellow NO MOTORIZED VEHICLES sign has been torn away and sailed off into the brush. All-terrain vehicle tracks, gouged a foot deep in the soft soil, lead down the slope, take a carefree U-turn, and come back up on the other side of the gate. Weaving waffle-tracks and long, deep, mudholes testify that this rare preserve has become a roarin', smokin' ATV superhighway.

It's not just the aesthetics, or even the rare orchids and other species in Crabtree Hollow that are at risk. Botanist Dan Boone, former director of the state's natural heritage program, says those big muddy tires are rolling the seeds of garlic mustard, knotweed, and stiltgrass right along into the middle of an as-yet uninvaded forest. They have already sprung up along the margins of the road.

Rick Barton is the DNR's director of state forests and parks. He regards the deer, the invasives, and the ATVs as serious threats to the forests and says they may well be addressed during forest management plan reviews in coming years. Among the range of possible solutions: more hunting, volunteer programs to treat invasives, and added law enforcement to stem the tide of ATVs.

Boone is skeptical, however: "Sure, we keep finding these little isolated patches of old growth. But we know we have one of the best old-growth forests in the mid-Atlantic here, and it doesn't have any real protection. It makes you wonder, what's the point of the old-growth survey? So we can identify more areas that we're not going to protect?"

Dombeck's Legacy

In the national forests, including those in Virginia, the high-water mark for protection of old growth was reached during the last few days of the Clinton administration. Then–Forest

Service chief Mike Dombeck appeared at a conference at Duke University on January 8, 2001, to say: "In the future, the Forest Service will manage old-growth forests specifically to maintain and enhance old-growth values and characteristics. . . . What we do not need to do to accomplish our stewardship responsibilities is to harvest old-growth trees."

The speech was widely reported as an ultimatum: no more old-growth logging. If so, and if it had stuck, this would have reversed current policy. It specifies that at times, old growth in national forests can be logged. That includes some of what may be as much as a quarter-million acres of old growth in the two Virginia national forests. Dombeck said the next day that he had been misunderstood, but a few weeks later, his resignation letter urged the incoming Bush administration that all old growth in the national forests—and hundreds of far larger "future old growth" roadless areas—be declared off-limits to roads and logging: "The greatest good for these remnant forests is found through their research and study, conservation and restoration."

Meanwhile, a bit of old growth may be cut for a new American Electric Power line that is likely to traverse the Jefferson National Forest in Virginia. The Hoover Creek timber sale on the Washington National Forest near Covington, Virginia, which included some old trees, was logged in 2002. Forest Service biologists said it wasn't an old-growth forest, but local environmentalists disagreed.

Old growth also figures in a new application by a Pittsburgh firm, the Equitable Production Company, to drill twenty-six natural gas wells and punch in about twenty-six miles of road on its leases in a roadless area near Pound, Virginia. Ninety-six percent of it is classified by the Forest Service as having "high existing scenic integrity." It includes 153 acres of "possible inventoried old growth" and three sites identified by the state natural heritage program as "biologically unique." A second company is preparing a proposal to develop natural gas on another 877 acres within the same roadless area.

Will this old growth, or Crabtree Hollow in Maryland, be logged someday? Highly unlikely, many forestry officials would say. By other reckonings, though, the reassurance rings hollow. Without permanent legal protection, promises about public lands sometimes only hold until the next election and a reassessment of the prevailing political breezes. Recent, abrupt policy changes to allow more logging on national forests testify that the public forests—old growth and future old growth alike—are to an unknown extent up for grabs.

Broader issues, at times just out of earshot, animate the old growth and "future old growth" debate and offer some basis for resolving it. For one, there's the distinction between private property and what is public—in the sense of being owned by all, in common:

"I think public lands ought to be managed for the goods and services that private lands either cannot or will not provide," says Dan Boone. "There's no economic incentive to manage for biological diversity, watershed protection, or remote recreational opportunities on private land. Private land is good for managing for timber."

Another such issue, fairness, is part of what grates on Del. George Edwards. Why should so much of the "future old growth" be in the western part of Maryland? Similar complaints are heard in the mountain counties of Virginia. "I'm glad I live here," Edwards jokes from his Garrett County office. "In five minutes I can be out in the middle of nowhere. You ought to have that opportunity, if you live in the Baltimore-Washington metro area." The state can buy some old farms there, he suggests, "and then if you let them sit long enough, you'll have an old-growth forest, too." Now there's a wry thought. Since it deflects discussion from the state forests that are already on the books, it's a bit of a red herring, too.

And yet not entirely: even as Edwards spoke, bulldozers were at work on a 235-acre, 132-unit residential development just across the road from the Belt Woods property. It could have served as a much-needed buffer for that coastal plain old-growth preserve—rarer by far, even, than mountain old growth.

A final broad-gauge issue might be thought of as civic self-restraint. Do we really have to log and road public forests, just to add to the national abundance of Kleenex and cardboard, furniture and shipping pallets?

Let Bill Damon, supervisor of Virginia's two national forests, have the last words on that. He has often parried such conflicts amid the shifting policies of his multiple-use, multiple-personality agency. Suitably, you can interpret his thoughts in at least a couple of ways:

"We have the most consumptive society in the world," he says. "If we can't figure out a way to environmentally, sustainably produce the forest products that we use from both our public and private lands, where are they going to come from? . . . To me, it's like we're a society that hasn't come to grips with the fact that there are limits."

Auguries

Undeterred by such thoughts, Jesse Overcash heads up the spine of a no-name ridge, several miles back in the woods from Wytheville, Virginia, navigating toward the old-growth forest he may have discerned on his seventy-year-old aerial photo. If so, it will add to the several thousand acres of old growth he has confirmed since beginning his part-time survey in 1989.

Thinking that we may be the first of our species to visit this ridge in a long time is a nice bonus. But here's a faint hunting trail, a cigarette butt, and a sun-faded Old Milwaukee can under a sassafras bush to dispel the illusion.

A mile over the ridge the shade deepens and the trail has vanished, though. No sane hunter would pursue a deer beyond the abrupt drop-off, or plan on grunting one back up if he bagged it. Overcash goes sliding and side-hilling. There are no stumps, no parted rocks hinting at dragged logs, no old roadbed.

And quickly, the trunks of great white, red, and chestnut oaks, tulip poplars, cucumber trees, basswoods, birch, Fraser magnolias, and red maples loom ahead. Grapevine festoons the crowns of standing dead trees. Maybe it was hard weather, the tough angle of the mountain, a dip in the construction economy back in the 1920s, the distraction of larger trees to cut nearby. One way or another, this remote place has eased past the inexorable efficiency of our great national sawmill. The trees here, mostly oaks, are big specimens.

We pause to lean against one old giant, with a coon-sized hollow and bark furrows as broad as a fist. Overcash uses a tape to measure another, a formidable oak that looms downslope, and it makes him whoop. It's 43.7 inches in diameter, huge for an upland tree in poor soil.

"This is the best stuff I've seen in a while," he says quietly. It may turn out to be a hundred acres or more, buffered by a much larger, if somewhat younger, forest. Using a T-handled auger that squawks with each turn into the wood, he pulls out a skinny core that gives off the strong, oaky fragrance of a high-dollar chardonnay. The ring count approximates 250 years—old growth for sure.

Overcash sits in the dirt and leaves, taking in the silent, massive girth of the trees around him. You could size them up as a series of handsome straight trunks, each of which might yield a couple of sixteen-foot logs for veneer or saw timber, he muses. You could see their potential as uncommonly good wildlife real estate, with hollows big enough to serve as bear condos.

Or you might imagine this tree as a thing distant in time, with as many centuries in its future as in its past. "Oh yeah!" he says with a laugh, bracing against the old oak to straighten up for the long hike out. "This is definitely a tree of debate!"

Memory Blanks: Notes on a New Civil War Campaign

The traffic's heavy as always on West Ox Road, one of dozens of feeder routes for the endless northern Virginia urbzone. A familiar din rises from the lattice of asphalt and strip malls, and reverberates off a twelve-story office building. Under blustery gray skies, Mario Espinola slowly canes his way off the sidewalk and into a few acres of forgotten pine woods, along a faint ridgeline path that leads back to nightfall on September 1, 1862.

Hidden in a tumble of downed trees and vines is the crest of the ridge, and a steep slope. There's so much thunder and lightning that soldiers say the storm scares them more than the artillery. It's deluge, darkness, and mud. The Twenty-first Massachusetts is in strange territory, heavily overgrown, and the men are disoriented.

They can't see over the lip of this ridge, and they are climbing into an ambush. When they breach the crest, a Confederate brigade looses a terrifying volley, sometimes from less than thirty feet away. A hundred Union soldiers fall.

In the melee that follows, the Union troops fire back, some abandoning their Enfield rifles to use backup revolvers. The Confederates are stunned by the speed and intensity of the return fire. But the natural advantage of the terrain allows them to stand their ground and eventually pursue the federals back to the road.

Henry Brown, a nineteen-year-old private with the Twenty-first, later wrote of the Battle of Ox Hill, of which this was a part, in a letter home: "It was a scene I shall never forget. It was wholesale murder to stand at the muzzle of the enemy's guns and have a volley poured into us. I had a very narrow escape of my life." (A Confederate shot, likely a Minié ball, had passed through his collar.)

At nearby Fairfax Station, Clara Barton was tending Union wounded. In her journal she wrote: "Of a sudden, air and earth and all about us shook with one mingled crash of God's and man's artillery. The lightning played and the thunder rolled incessantly and the cannon roared louder and nearer each minute. . . . With what desperation our men fought hour after hour in the rain and darkness!"

Mario Espinola has reconstructed this scene from the evidence of excavated buttons, bullets, and percussion caps, from years of measuring impact zones, reading diaries and official records, and collecting oral histories. Almost nothing within the three hundred acres of the Battle of Ox Hill has been preserved during the development boom that began here in the late 1980s, though, despite the efforts of people like Espinola, who over the past quarter century has researched the battle, documented the obliteration of the site, and protested the development.

Somewhere nearby, a couple of chain saws are snarling. Where the woods meet the road, there's a sign bearing notice of a public hearing on plans to develop this parcel. For Espinola, it's an old story. "I was wondering when that was going to happen," he says. Ox Hill was showcased as an example, by a national study commission, of a battle site that has been "truly obliterated." In fact, this is becoming an old story across many of the nation's remaining Civil War battlefields, which often include archaeological data that could illuminate a key chapter in our national history.

Frank McManamon, chief archaeologist for the National Park Service, has watched the progress of these disappearances during his twenty-five-year career with the Interior Department. "It's pretty constant that these things come up," he says.

"The resource is finite. It's being used up. Unless there is some sort of preservation scheme for the landscapes and the sites that they are embedded in, they will be lost."

The Civil War wasn't fought in parks but on private land, and most of it still remains in private hands. Only a handful of battle sites are owned principally by federal or other public agencies. There is no national policy on Civil War battlefield preservation. Instead, there's a helter-skelter, high-stakes, and often high-volume debate among local and national interests: landowners, real estate developers, Civil War reenactors, relic hunters, open space advocates, history buffs, highway construction lobbyists, tourism promoters, preservationists, the Sons of Union Veterans, and United Daughters of the Confederacy, to cite a few of the players.

And the verdict of decision-makers in scores of places across the United States has been that archaeology, history, education, commemoration, and open green space are not necessarily the highest and best uses for valuable land. There is also a concerted effort, in which archaeology often plays a significant role, to push back. In deceptively simple terms, they are debating these questions: how much land do you save, and how much are you willing to spend to save it?

The same real estate development surge that erased history at Ox Hill also threatened a big chunk of the nearby but better-known Second Manassas battlefield more than ten years ago. By the time the government made up its mind to protect that site from a proposed shopping mall, the price tag for the buyout had become spectacularly high: $120 million for four-hundred-odd acres. In the wake of that debacle, Congress set up a special commission to catalog and prioritize Civil War battlefields, so they might be purchased before urbanization and speculation jacked the asking prices out of reach.

In its 1993 report, the congressional commission catalogued 10,500 Civil War battle and skirmish sites, tagging 384 of them as "principal battlefields." It concluded: "This nation's Civil War heritage is in grave danger. . . . More than one-third of

all principal Civil War battlefields are either lost or are hang-
ing onto existence by the slenderest of threads. . . . Within
ten years we may lose fully two-thirds of the principal battlefields."

Those ten years have passed. Instead of the $90 million that
the commission recommended be spent for land acquisitions
during that period, only some $20 million was appropriated
and spent. How much has been lost since 1993 won't be clear
until a new study by the National Park Service is completed in
a couple of years, but tens of thousands of acres is a safe estimate.

As with any cause where emotions run high, it's well to
remember that the other side has some reasonable points to
make, too. Here's a paraphrase of an argument that is usually
on offer when a battle site is "in play":

Of course we should honor the sacrifices made in the Civil
War, or in any other part of our national history, and we have
a lot of ways to do that. But locking up more land cramps the
economy and stifles the creation of new jobs. This mania for
preserving whole landscapes—it's something like that apocryphal tribe of highly religious natives that depended on river
fishing for its survival. One day someone got the bright idea
that the gods had declared all the fishing canoes taboo. So the
whole tribe starved to death.

Here's another perspective on whether too much land might
be sequestered from the national economy if battlefields are
protected:

- The federal commission's list of 384 significant battlefields
  represents only 3.7 percent of the total list of Civil War
  battle and skirmish sites.
- That 3.7 percent was prioritized further, into four catego-
  ries, based on a site's significance, condition, and the degree to which it is threatened.
- For argument's sake, just lop off the bottom-priority cate-
  gory, and consider only the remaining 249 sites. They rep-

resent some 280,000 acres. For comparison, that's about a quarter of the size of the average single U.S. national forest. And there are 155 national forests.

- Of those 280,000 acres of battlefields we've whittled things down to, the nonprofit Civil War Preservation Trust (CWPT) figures it will be very lucky to preserve less than 10 percent over the coming decade.

Whether that looks like a bid to save everything and lock it up forever, as critics sometimes claim, depends on your point of view. Doing even that much, however, would require about $50 million from Congress, and an equal amount from state, local, and private sources. (For comparison, the total is about the same amount of money it took to produce the Hollywood Civil War epic *Cold Mountain*.)

Preservation advocates often point out that tourism dollars make big economic ripples, justifying more acquisitions. A recent analysis sponsored by the CWPT looked at a handful of both lesser-known and nationally known battlefield parks. At Kentucky's Mill Springs, 4,300 annual battle-site visitors support four full-time jobs, generate $83,000 in other local income, and yield $25,000 in local and state tax revenues.

At the other end of the scale, there's Gettysburg National Military Park: 1.6 million visitors, 2,653 full-time jobs, $52.2 million in local income, and $17 million in local and state tax revenues. Whether this outranks the potential income from roads, houses, office parks, or strip-mining that Civil War battlefields might also be used for is another matter, since each local economy and each site are unique. The unquantifiable part of the equation is, what price tag do you hang on your own national heritage?

The impact is more than regional. Much of the Civil War was fought outside the South. Important battlefields are scattered through twenty-six states from New Mexico to Florida. "It's not like we're out of the picture. It's not like only a little bit happened out here in the Midwest," says Douglas Scott, an archaeologist at the Park Service's Midwest Archaeological Center in Lincoln, Nebraska. Missouri, for example, had some 1,500 Civil War battles and skirmishes—only outranked by Virginia and Tennessee.

And battlefields at Pea Ridge, Arkansas, or Pilot Knob, Missouri, are also in the path of change that can determine the future of the landscape and foreclose the discovery of its past. "It is a concern here, as it is in so many areas," Scott says. "What was once essentially farmland that nobody thought was ever going to change is being built upon by people who want to get out of the main city and live on a nice little acreage of some sort. I think the interest is there to preserve and document many of these sites, but whether the resources are there, I don't know. I am very concerned that our losses are going to be cumulative, and the more we lose, the less we are going to understand about the past."

Scott says he's a realist. Not everything can be saved. But in the discussion of priorities that occurs in all communities, he wants to make sure that citizens at least come to know what they may be losing. "People tell me we've got enough bottles, or enough bullets or enough nails. Sure, we have a lot of examples of what was used in the past, from specific sites, and they will tell us a lot about that site . . . but it's about putting all the information from a site together—historical records, oral histories, and the archaeological record—to understand the event on that particular piece of land."

Archaeology yields clues that can help resolve larger historical issues. For example, the accepted wisdom has been that British Enfield and Austrian muskets were not used in the West in 1861, and barely in 1862, because the government wasn't buying and shipping them out there. But recently, Scott says, physical evidence including bullets has been found showing that the guns were there. This is probably because local militia units on both sides were arming themselves using private funds, well before the war. This was a heavily armed population, even then.

"Archaeology gives a broader scale, a better picture of the logistics, supply, command, and control that existed before the Civil War," Scott says. "The historical record provides us one set of records and the archaeological data provides another. Combined, they tell a much truer story of the past."

The details that come out of the ground are also the spark with which a personal connection can, on a lucky day, be forged with the past. It's currently our best and only means of time travel: a harmonica from a soldier's pocket, a button off the coat, the broken hilt of a saber.

"Most of these battlefields have a unique history. It's not like you are hearing the same story time after time," says Jim Campi, a CWPT spokesman. "Archaeologically, too, these sites have a story to tell. When you go to the history books, a lot of what soldiers said in battle reports can't be understood unless you can go out and see the site, and see the folds in the land, why decisions were made the way they were because of the contours of the battlefield.

"So much can be taught on these battlefields. Not every community has a Chancellorsville in its backyard. But they do have Wilson's Creek in Missouri, and Franklin in Tennessee, or the battlefields around Mobile, Alabama."

Some nights over Shreveport, the headquarters for another battlefield controversy, there's a hint of the local refinery in the air—like swamp vapor crossed with Vaseline.

Backcountry Louisiana comes right up to the outskirts of town, lapping at the edges of the due-south freeway. Forty miles distant, past brushfields, oaks shrouded in kudzu, and small, lone houses under pleated awnings and tin roofs, is the sleepy hamlet of Mansfield.

This was the scene of the northernmost battle of the Union army and navy's Red River campaign in early April 1864, and arguably the last major Confederate victory of the war. The federals brought forty thousand men up the river in ninety iron-clad, tin-clad, and cotton-clad boats to try to take Shreveport.

But the boats were nearly stranded in low water, the Yank army was routed, and the campaign, says Civil War historian Gary Joiner, was "a pretty dismal thing, primarily because the Union General Nathaniel Banks was inept. On his best day, he was inept."

At Mansfield and other sites, new technology is part of the preservationist's tool kit. Joiner is also a geographer and has worked at several Civil War sites using geographic information system (GIS) maps. These are visual displays of multiple layers of data on, for example, battle lines, archaeological finds, creeks, and fences or houses from the Civil War period. Those layers are overlain by others, showing contemporary data on property ownerships, existing buildings, and parcels that might be available for purchase. The resulting picture often clarifies priorities: what's important historically, where there are likely to be undisturbed archaeological deposits, what's available for protection, and who owns it.

At the Battle of Mansfield, the most significant events took place on something like 1,500 acres of ground, and much of the battlefield looks today as it did then. But that's changing abruptly. Only 180 acres are protected as a state commemorative area, and underlying the battlefield is a broad seam of lignite coal. Two enormous coal shovels have already strip-mined thousands of acres, operating with a kind of ponderous precision, hollowing out the land to a depth of about twenty feet, and producing 3 million tons of lignite each year to feed a power plant whose stacks are visible on the southern horizon.

The Southwestern Electric Power Company, a subsidiary of American Electric Power of Columbus, Ohio, says its mining at Mansfield is "practiced responsibly, in accordance with the wishes of those who own the property and in compliance with all federal and state laws." It argues that its strip mine helps keep down the cost of electric power in the region and provides employment for 173 people earning an annual payroll of $10 million.

"Nobody working on this issue wants to harm jobs or the power plant," Joiner counters. "They've got thousands and thousands of acres of a good coal seam. All we're saying is, leave what is historically important." Joiner teaches military history at a local university, and his complex GIS mapping systems have guided archaeological excavations here, at Gettysburg, and at Petersburg. He says the mining has already converted about 20 percent of the battle site—the knolls, dells, and streams cited in diaries, letters, and the official record of the battle, as well as the archaeological record—into a flat, pulverized moonscape.

Joiner also has evidence for what he says may be a burial site for three dozen soldiers, not far from where the coal company is operating and in part of its leasehold. Joiner and the group he organized just last year, the three-hundred-strong Friends of Mansfield Battlefield—mostly locals, but now some business and organizational members throughout the United States and even in Europe—are challenging the mine before state and federal authorities, and courting landowners.

"History, to a lot of folks, is important until the dollar sign gets in the way," Joiner says. "Then it's like any other sensitive archaeological site. I've worked on a bunch of them, and this is a poster child for it."

Are there important archaeological opportunities at Mansfield? "Yes, absolutely. In fact, we have enough information together that I was able to file two archaeological site forms with the State of Louisiana, on potential mass Union graves in the line of the strip-mine drag-line.

"I'm a conservative, I'm a Republican. I'm pro-business. But there comes a time when you have to have a social conscience. At some point we have to figure out, as a culture, that everything does not belong in a big box—Wal-Mart or Home Depot. You have to save something so that the generations that come after us will have something to talk about.

"This is not a Confederate thing, it's not a Union thing, it's an American thing. If we don't protect this land, who's going to protect it? Who will be the guardians of American history if the American people don't do it? It's going to have to be protected from guys in three-piece suits in boardrooms, making decisions about what *they* consider to be important and unimportant on a local, regional, and national scale."

Joiner is dukes-up, says he is in it for the long haul and confident of victory: "There's a fine old southern tradition called being cold-cocked. It's particularly fun for people who are arrogant. Sometimes you just have to pick your fights. This is my fight. This is it. I live here."

During one night of "Stoneman's raid"—a long and punishing foray into the South in the spring of 1865—the namesake Union general marched his army right through the center of tiny Bethania, North Carolina. "The oral tradition in one family," says archaeologist Michael Hartley, "is that a most memorable sight in the life of one of their women was the glint of moonlight on the bayonets of Stoneman's infantry on its march up the street."

Relief was intense that Stoneman left Bethania intact. "They had pressed a Negro of the town to pilot them to the Shallowford on the Yadkin," a local diarist noted. "The army left between 11–12 o'clock, doing us no further harm, for which we felt thankful to the Lord." It was April 10, the day after Lee's surrender at Appomattox.

So there was no battle here, but then archaeology is not only about battlefields and the dead. The war's end powerfully deflected the paths of the living—not least, the black people of Bethania. Their descendants still remain in the area, and some have a keen sense that reconstructing the past is essential in trying to comprehend their own lives.

Hartley came to know Bethania when it lay in the path of a superhighway project. He began the archaeology that ended with the redirection of the highway and the inclusion of part of the town in the National Historic Register. A Moravian settlement that dates from 1759, its archaeological record is now under the shadow of a new threat: the explosive growth of the city of Winston-Salem, just down the road. New homes are going up on the back lanes of the picturesque little town and out on country roads where most of the black population lives.

"I think that Bethania is an immense database for the presence of African Americans on the landscape, enslaved and free, and that is an interesting contrast," he says. "Because of the presence of their descendants, there is a whole continuum to be examined from the inception of slavery to its end, and after that into the present."

Archaeology could explore, for example, how relationships played out between white Moravians—some of whom opposed slavery for religious reasons—and their slaves, who were also Moravians, during and after the war. That is, if their traces do not disappear under proposed new roads and housing subdivisions.

A nearby site offering plenty of archaeological opportunity is a crossroads called Washington Town, a free black settlement established in the 1830s. "What kinds of dynamics began to act on these people as the war ended?" Hartley asks. "We know that African American schools began to spring up in the late nineteenth century, and that could be explored."

Georgia Byrd knows about one such school, and wishes she knew more. It is nearly gone now—just a scatter of bricks next to a stream under a bridge. After the Civil War ended, schools were something like the epicenter for black aspirations. Byrd and her brother have been working, with severely limited means, to interest local government in initiating some archaeological investigations and protecting at least some of the landscape. The school site suggests itself. "We had a school there, and somehow, we let it go. We didn't know how to hold onto that history," she says.

Byrd lives in a trailer east of Bethania, near what used to be called the Great Philadelphia Wagon Road. "Every black family on this road can pretty much trace their roots back to the time when their parents worked for the white settlers. My great- great- great-ancestors were some of the first to purchase land as free black persons, right after the war. My grandmother used to tell me the people just tented out up here." On an overgrown adjacent parcel, her grandmother also used to say, are the remains of her great uncles.

"Real estate people tell their clients, just don't believe those people, they're crazy. But we're not lying. We're not just making up these stories. These are facts. When people live on the land this long, a hundred years, there has to be some history someplace."

Byrd and Hartley both seek in Civil War–era archaeology something like an antidote to the onset of a cultural Alzheimer's: "We want to say wait a minute, we have a history, too," Byrd says. "We want to leave a legacy here. Don't just bulldoze us down and say we never existed. We've done a lot. I guarantee there's something. An old slave tag. The heel of a shoe. We just know we're ready for it. We're just coming into ourselves to realize the worth, the value, the history that we have here."

Hartley's view is similar: "It's not about boxes of things stuck back on a shelf, but how to translate them into some meaningful information about ourselves. The stories that are not of the immediate present—that don't come at us out of MTV."

He's heard the "who cares?" questions about digging up old artifacts many times. "It is very easy for us to lose our way when we ask what is the significance of this or that. I would respond well, how many subdivisions do we need? How many four-, five-, or eight-lane highways do we need, and how much good are those things doing us now, as we begin to consider how we impose ourselves on the landscape?"

At times the National Park Service has done an outstanding job of protecting already existing battlefields within its domain from the incursions of uncomprehending pressure groups. But the federal role in enlarging protected areas—limited always by available funds—also depends heavily on local sentiment.

The government loathes to involve itself where local support is lacking. To employ a battlefield metaphor that is also a cliché: this can be a two-edged sword.

One of the great success stories in Civil War battlefield archaeology preservation is occurring now, with the creation of the Moccasin Bend National Archaeological District along the Tennessee River. It will be added to nine-thousand-acre Chickamauga and Chattanooga National Military Park, the scene of an epic contest in 1863 involving more than one hundred thousand troops, when the Confederates attempted, in vain, to stop the Union advance on Chattanooga, a major rail and supply center.

Chattanooga archaeologist Lawrence Alexander notes that the Park Service, constrained by limited budgets and other priorities, initially opposed the idea. Pressure channeled through an enthusiastic and well-connected local Republican congressman, Zach Wamp, who serves on the House Appropriations Committee, forced its hand.

The same armies clashed a hundred miles north, at Murfreesboro, Tennessee, but there the preservation story line turns upside down. At Stone's River National Battlefield, local pressure has led to commercial development of land that the Park Service had earmarked as crucial to understanding the December 31, 1862–January 2, 1863, battle, which involved eighty thousand troops and resulted in twenty-four thousand casualties. A lone victory during a bleak time for the Union military, it was a turning point Lincoln was able to capitalize on to maintain support for the war. The current park includes seven hundred acres—less than 20 percent of the battlefield.

"The proposed development land is where most of the Confederate units were positioned during the Battle of Stone's River," a preservation-minded citizen wrote the *Nashville Tennessean* of one construction project. "Can you imagine this taking place next door to the Gettysburg National Battlefield, or the Saint Laurent Cemetery in Normandy, France?"

Jim Ogden, the historian at Chickamauga and Chattanooga

National Military Park, has worked on many archaeological digs in the region and visits Stone's River a couple of times a year. "Every time I go, another portion of the battlefield has disappeared to some development," he says. "The [local] government there is even working to build a big medical campus on a portion of the historic battlefield, as we speak. The bulldozers are pushing the dirt." House sites, fence lines, and property lines that might have helped refine our understanding of that battle are disappearing, Ogden says. Speaking only for himself, he poses a question: "Has the National Park Service been proactive enough to be ahead of these threats? My answer to that is no."

Archaeology can supply data that are often missing from war records, newspaper stories, and personal accounts, even where these historical records about a particular battle are plentiful. But advances in archaeological techniques in recent years can't be used on sites that are sold off and paved before they're reconnoitered, notes Park Service archaeologist David Orr, who is also on the faculty at Temple University. For example: working with Orr, Park Service archaeologists Doug Campana and Julie Steele and geophysicist Bruce Bevan measured electrical resistance and magnetism in the soils around Fort Morton at the Petersburg, Virginia, battlefield. They also employed ground-penetrating radar. In a field, they located the fort itself, the "bombproof" shelters within the fort, battle trenches, a well full of iron artifacts, and a house near the outer fortifications. "It's a very important fort in the siege of Petersburg," he says. "We found it in only three or four days."

To protect such places if there is local support, the Park Service's American Battlefield Protection Program (ABPP) provides seed money as well as organizational and research expertise. It has a staff of just four, and a half-million dollars a year for grants. That amount covered only about a third of the eligible requests for help last year. The program politely excuses itself from the role of outside agitator in local fights over battle sites. Its job is to find ways to preserve them without having to spend federal money buying them.

"The good news is that something is available to citizens to take advantage of," says Frank McManamon, the top federal archaeologist. But while the government provides some tools and modest funding, local initiative, he points out, is pivotal. And that's one of the lessons suggested by these fights over Civil War landscapes: Despite some federal help and the work of private, state, and national groups such as the CWPT, a grassroots effort is indispensable for many preservation projects, especially in their initial stages.

The second point, the one archaeology can make most strongly, is that this enterprise is more than just a hobby for history buffs or a narrow academic quest. The details that come out of the ground are, advocates say, one of the few ways future generations can hope to come to grips with the meaning of a war on our own land, among our own citizens, that cost 620,000 lives.

When Kristen Stevens, staff archaeologist for the ABPP, worked at the Gettysburg National Military Park a few years ago, some human remains were discovered along a railroad cut. The analysis was tenuous. "We based most of our observations on the slimmest of evidence, just the shadows of what was on the human remains and the bones—an undershirt button and the heel of a shoe," Stevens recalls. "To me, it really heightened the importance of every scrap of evidence. Every Minié ball counts."

The episode reminded her, once again, of the taproot for battlefield preservation—and even, perhaps, for archaeology itself. "People were hounding us. They were riveted, trying to figure out whose family that soldier might have belonged to, which side he might have represented. It's a compelling thing. I think it's just a matter of wanting to identify. You want to really understand that person's story. Why was he here? And I guess the biggest question rolls into that: why are we here?"

Rough Mountain, &
Associates

Forty-four thousand people sought the great outdoors in Shenandoah National Park during the long Independence Day weekend, but a couple of hours to the south, in the thirty-nine square miles of the state's newest wilderness areas, almost no one showed up.

The promise of solitude is one reason federal legislators endorsed the Virginia Wilderness Act, which set aside four additional woodland tracts in southwest Virginia, enlarging the designated wilderness in the state's national forests by nearly 50 percent.

"I'm not a big hiker," said Forest Service spokeswoman Marty Longan, an Arlington resident. "But it's nice to know that it's there, when I'm sitting in the middle of traffic on I-395." Advocates also argued that rare plants and a variety of animals would find refuge in the protected areas, and that the wilderness is a living symbol of American ideals. "The wilderness resources are the reason the colonists came to the New World four hundred years ago," said Ed Clark, director of the Wildlife Center of Virginia at Weyer's Cave. "That's every bit as much a part of our history and heritage as the Washington Monument. It is, in a sense, a living legacy that we can leave for future generations, so that they can understand the foundations on which our history has been built."

The federal legislation added four areas to Virginia's eleven wildernesses:

- Rough Mountain, 9,300 acres of mixed oaks and Virginia pine on steep shale slopes in Bath County, near Clifton Forge.
- Rich Hole, 6,450 acres in Alleghany and Rockbridge counties northwest of Lexington, with rocky outcrops providing views of nearby North Mountain and Simpson's Creek Valley.
- Barbour's Creek, 5,700 acres in Craig County.
- Shawver's Run, 3,665 acres in Craig and Alleghany counties. Barbour's Creek and Shawver's Run lie along Potts Mountain, northwest of New Castle. There are no trails in the Shawver's Run Wilderness, so hiking is all cross-country. Rough Mountain and Rich Hole are part of the George Washington National Forest, and Barbour's Creek and Shawver's Run are in the Jefferson National Forest.

The wilderness act also added 72 acres to the Lewis Fork Wilderness on the flank of Mount Rogers in Grayson County to adjust a boundary, and added 2,500 acres in Monroe County, West Virginia, to the Mountain Lake Wilderness.

The preserves are the product of nearly a decade of negotiation among environmentalists, the logging industry, legislators, local government, and the U.S. Forest Service. The four sites were granted temporary protection as "wilderness study areas" when the state's other wilderness areas were set aside in 1984. The exclusion resulted from opposition by the Westvaco Corp., whose mill in Covington manufactures bleached paperboard and employs 1,700. The company feared that wilderness areas in the vicinity of its mill might result in tightened air-quality standards that could block expansion plans.

Westvaco dropped its objections, however, saying that its own air-quality studies and reassurance from the bill's sponsors—Reps. James R. Olin (D-Va.) and Frederick C. (Rick) Boucher (D-Va.)—had eased its fears.

The change of official status is gradually visible along the only trail that traverses the Barbour's Creek wilderness. Knee-high sassafras and oak already obscure a jeep track once used to stock Lipes Branch creek with hatchery-bred trout. Roads and motor vehicles are banned from wilderness areas, and the streams will be left to native trout.

A few fallen trees block the steeply ascending trail, but when Forest Service maintenance crews come through, they won't bring chain saws and bulldozers. No motorized equipment is permitted, so they will use the two-handled cross-cut saws they call "misery whips." All commercial logging is now forbidden, and trees will begin to reclaim areas that were harvested as recently as 1975.

Hunting for deer, bear, and turkey, which is allowed in wilderness areas during designated seasons, is excellent, according to biologist Alan Guthrie of the state's Department of Game and Inland Fisheries. Some local hunters were numbered among the supporters of the legislation.

"I wanted it," said Harry Crawford of New Castle, who loads up his bear dogs and rifle three or four times a year to go hunting around Barbour's Creek or Shawver's Run. "They've got too many roads, too much access to this country," he said. Hunters who rely on the roads tend to "kill everything they see. . . . We figured [the wilderness status] would save the bear and the other game, too."

Forest Service personnel say that all but a small fraction of the visitors to the new wilderness areas come during deer- and bear-hunting seasons, roughly from Thanksgiving to the week after New Year's. Bob Boardwine, district ranger in the Jefferson National Forest, estimates that fewer than two hundred hikers and equestrians visit Barbour's Creek every year.

The Forest Service expects more people to visit. "The fact that it is labeled 'wilderness' is going to elevate the use to some extent," said Frank Bergmann, a Forest Service planner for Rough Maintain, the largest of the new preserves. "We don't really know what could happen."

Rough Mountain is home to several plants rare in Virginia,

such as Kate's mountain clover, western wallflower, mountain pimpernel, northern bedstraw, white-haired leather flower, and twin grass, said Michael Lipford, director of the state's National Heritage Program. It also shelters the shale barren rock cress, a species so rare it has been proposed for federal listing as threatened, and state listing as endangered.

Bergmann said he plans to solicit public comment on what, if anything, should be done next at Rough Mountain. The sole trail over Rough Mountain passes through a wilderness larger than Tyson's Corner and Vienna put together, ending at a point near the Calf Pasture River. The trail may be maintained, it could be allowed to vanish as the seasons pass, or new trails could be added.

A similar planning process, trying to balance human use with wilderness values, will be under way soon for each of the four new areas. "What it comes down to is the limits of acceptable change in the wilderness," Bergmann said.

If change arrives at Rich Hole, one of its agents will be Bill Simmons of Covington, a retired computer programmer who is now a volunteer scout for the Forest Service. With map, compass, and altimeter, he already has marked potential new trails up the hollows and along the spine of Brush Mountain. In two years of hiking the area, he has come upon other visitors only once. "After all, it's very difficult walking," he said. "When I ask people to go with me, they don't want to.

"I've been 'attacked' by these little bitty grouse who have chicks. I'll be walking along and all of a sudden this ball of feathers comes roaring at me. One came within six inches of my feet and stopped to look at me. See, I didn't run like I was supposed to." Simmons also has come across the remains of old iron mines, mining equipment, and railroad grades on the mountain.

Rich Hole is notable for its patches of virgin timber, remote enough to have escaped logging that began in the area more than a century ago. Hemlocks and tulip poplars more than three feet in diameter have been found along Alum Creek, said wilderness advocate Ernest Dickerman of Buffalo Gap. "For a national forest in the East, that's a big tree," he said. Dickerman was among those who lobbied for the creation of the state wilderness system.

The wild character of Rich Hole was exemplified during a July 2 "wilderness celebration" sponsored by Olin. He and Dickerman led celebrants on a hike along the creek and up the ridge, but stragglers lost their way and had to retrace their steps as the footpath quickly faded amid thick underbrush.

Wolves of Isle Royale

It's cold this winter at Isle Royale National Park. Out on Lake Superior between Minnesota and northern Michigan, temperatures can drop to 30 below. Snow, two feet deep in an average year, softens the contours of the ice-locked lakes, scarped ridges, and bone-white aspen. The eastern timber wolves that roam the island are well adapted for such extremes. Their thick winter pelage is proof against the cold, and moose kills are cooperative, efficient.

Only a few wolf tracks cross the snowfields now, however. The Isle Royale population has "crashed," as biologists put it, from a peak of fifty in 1980 to twelve in 1988. No one knows why.

An array of research projects is under way to probe the riddle of the wolves' decline, and national park administrators are weighing their options. At least two of these scientific and management questions foreshadow situations that other national parks, and many natural preserves around the world, will face during the next decades.

At times, the National Park Service and other agencies face a conflict between protecting natural ecological processes and saving threatened wildlife populations. These conflicts revolve around a newly pressing question: What does "natural" mean?

Protecting small populations of an endangered species may not suffice. If the species is to have a fighting chance for survival, some genetic variability must also be preserved.

Isle Royale, the serene backdrop for these difficult issues, is the kind of laboratory wildlife biologists dream of but seldom encounter. Its 210 square miles are isolated in the vastness of the world's largest body of fresh water, Lake Superior.

The island's ecology is thus simpler and more self-contained than on the mainland, and predator-prey relationships unfold with greater clarity. Even more important, the impact of *Homo sapiens* has been extraordinarily restrained at Isle Royale during the last half century. The park is roadless and open to visitors only six-and-a-half months a year. Under these auspicious conditions, two generations of scientists have studied the lifeways of seven generations of wolves, and the wolves have enjoyed something akin to a state of grace. Though a stream of articles and books have made them the most studied and most publicized of their kind, Isle Royale's wolves were the last known anywhere in the United States whose lives in the wilderness were not troubled by direct human contact.

Even the scientists took their notes from high above, during thirty winters of queasy circles in light planes. On the ground, they patiently collected and then analyzed moose carcasses and wolf scat, rather than the animals themselves. The luxury of this scientific distance vanished during the past summer, however, after the wolf population's near-extinction had forced the issue. A team led by Rolf Peterson, a wildlife ecologist at Michigan Technological University, trapped and tranquilized four of the wolves, then released them after taking blood samples. Also, for the first time, they fitted the wolves with radio collars. Mortality sensors in the collars will allow the scientists to retrieve—for autopsy—any of the four that die.

"A lot of us wish we didn't really have to do this, that we could allow the process to continue without our getting involved in it," said Robert Krumenaker, the park's resource-management specialist, while the trapping effort was under way. "Many of us feel like we're losing something philosophically when we have to go in and handle the wolves, the symbols of wilderness out here."

Peterson has studied Isle Royale's wolves for eighteen years, but because his research proposal reversed the long-standing park policy against direct contact, it was circulated among twenty administrators and scientists both within and outside of the National Park Service before it was funded and allowed to go forward. Concerned that the island's entire wolf population would be wiped out, Peterson had few doubts about intervening. "When the specter of extinction is fully realized, you've got to push these minor concerns aside," he says. "The greatest tragedy would be if they disappeared and we didn't even know why. Then you'd really be in the dark in terms of what to do next."

Peterson is supervising research that is a collaborative effort of scientists from Canada to California. It's designed to investigate the three most likely reasons for the wolf population's sudden collapse: food scarcity, inbreeding, and disease. Two or even three of these possibilities may be interacting, and each is bound up with the relatively brief history of wolves and moose on the island.

Moose arrived from Canada soon after the turn of the twentieth century, though what caused their migration is unknown. They are strong swimmers, even in the forbidding chill of Lake Superior. With no natural predators to control their numbers, the moose population may have reached 2,500 or more by the mid-1930s, far exceeding the island's capacity to support them. A typical moose consumes an estimated 3.65 tons of vegetation a year. Predictably, the uncontrolled moose population stripped the island of the available food supply. A catastrophic die-off claimed all but a few hundred of the animals, and observers speculated that even those might starve. Carcasses littered the island, and the smell reached park visitors arriving in the spring.

But the remnant herd was spared, thanks to huge fires that burned nearly a quarter of the island in 1936, allowing new "moose salad" to grow. The moose population's slow buildup toward starvation began again.

Sometime during the winter of 1949, however, an ice bridge formed between the island and the mainland, and a pack of wolves made the crossing, probably from Ontario's Sibley Peninsula fifteen miles away. They found a sanctuary free of their principal predators—men with guns—and a moose population ripe for harvest, and they prospered.

One of the most significant findings of the long-term Isle Royale wolf study has been the beneficial nature, for moose as well as wolves, of this predator-prey relationship. Thousands of hours of observation have confirmed that the wolves are masters at culling the old, the young, and the sickly from among the moose herd.

Indeed, though moose meat is 80 percent of their diet, the wolves must be extremely selective, or they court death. After it is a year old, the average, gentle-faced moose has no trouble deploying its hooves, antlers, and nine-hundred-pound bulk in formidable, and usually successful, self-defense. Wolves often face fractured ribs and worse in an encounter with a healthy moose.

So the wolves limited the moose herd, the forage regenerated, and the herd became healthier. Both species were able to attain a higher population density than recorded anywhere else. One theory of wolf dynamics suggested that, because of a strong sense of territory, wolves could not reach an average density greater than one per ten square miles. But, as Isle Royale's population grew to twice that number, it became apparent that food availability, more than territoriality, determines population density.

Given a stable environment, Peterson speculated, the cycle in which first prey, then predator, populations rise and fall on the island is roughly thirty to forty years. Thus, under pressure from a burgeoning wolf population, the moose herd thinned by the late 1970s. "In terms of their basic estate, the wolves spent the annual earnings of interest and were digging into the principal," wrote Durward Allen, the Purdue University biologist and self-described old-timer who founded the wolf study.

Vulnerable moose were increasingly rare. The wolves, numerous and hungry, began to turn on each other, yielding yet another significant finding. Wolves, it seems, have evolved social behavior that regulates their number when food becomes scarce. Deadly territorial conflict between packs increases, and reproduction decreases.

From 1980 to 1982, fifty wolves diminished to fourteen, and the moose population moved upward in the expected natural counterpoint. In two more years the wolves had rebounded to twenty-four, about the average. But by the winter of 1987–88, the wolves had declined again to only a dozen, and scientists could not say why. Concern deepened that the wolves might all be gone before long. The research proposal was approved. "If we find that the wolves' only problem is starvation," Peterson told a reporter, "the most common public response will be: 'Feed 'em.'"

Supplemental feeding would, of course, mean an even greater departure from the park's policy of noninterference with natural ecological processes. For these wolves, however, that issue may be moot. The blood samples are being tested for levels of various nutrients, but the two males and two females Peterson trapped were larger than expected. Wolves are usually lean, he says, but "these guys were heavy."

Krumenaker described one as "an incredibly healthy-looking animal. She was beautiful. She had a fantastic coat. She seemed to be fit and have about the right amount of fat. She wasn't skin and bone. There was nothing visibly wrong with this animal. So food may or may not explain everything we're seeing."

Wolf watchers had wondered whether some factor other than the food supply might be at work, and Peterson had designed the research plan with that question in mind. The blood samples were to be tested for several diseases, especially parvovirus. A disease that attacks canine digestive tracts, parvovirus has decimated populations of domestic dogs and captive wolves.

Isle Royale's isolation has been a partial barrier to mainland flora and fauna. But, as with the migrations of wolf and moose, chance and opportunity present the possibility for contamination. Most human visitors to the island embark on boats at Houghton or Copper Harbor, on Michigan's Upper Peninsula, about fifty miles and four to six hours away. According to veterinarians there, parvo reached epidemic levels in Houghton in 1981, which coincides with the period of the wolves' most drastic decline. In that year, no wolf pups survived on the island.

"Parvo tends to kill pups really young, really fast," Krumenaker said. "Dogs, cats, and other mammals are prohibited from entering the park, but that doesn't mean it doesn't happen. Every year we find a few. We insist that those people [with animals] leave the park, but the damage could conceivably be done."

Tests for parvo antibodies showed conclusively that the disease made it to the island at some time in the past, and thus cannot be ruled out as the cause of the wolves' decline. On the other hand, although an all-or-none result had been expected, only two of the four wolves tested positive for parvo. These signals were so enigmatic that the tests were run a second time, with identical results.

The next possibility researchers are exploring involves the wolves' genetic predicament. Isle Royale's small contingent of *Canis lupus* is an island community in more than the obvious way. Its isolation cuts off the wolf pack from larger, ancestral gene pools in Minnesota and Canada. As populations of countless other wild species are fragmented, isolated, and severely diminished by the competitive pressure of humans, these populations, too, will become genetic "islands."

If the members of these surviving groups are too closely related, chances increase that offspring will inherit maladaptive genes from both parents, a phenomenon called "inbreeding depression." Its most prominent symptoms are low reproductive capacity, high infant mortality, and low resistance to disease.

Cheetahs, for example, have always been difficult to breed in captivity. A series of experiments have shown that the world's twenty thousand remaining cheetahs are astonishingly homo-genetic—almost as similar as siblings. This genetic similarity is evidence that, at one or at several times in the past, only a small number of cheetahs were alive to pass along their genetic legacy. Sperm counts for tested cheetahs were extremely low, and 71 percent of the spermatozoa were misshapen, compared to about 29 percent in domestic cats. Cheetahs also seem to suc-cumb to diseases that other related species are able to survive.

Condors, Asiatic elephants, black-footed ferrets, Florida pan-thers, and countless other "island" species may be vulnerable to the ill effects of inbreeding depression because of narrowed genetic variability. For that reason, the Isle Royale blood sam-ples will be elaborately analyzed for clues to any genetic prob-lems among the wolves—the first time such work has been done on this species.

On the other hand, Peterson notes, though the current work should add considerably to the fund of data, our knowledge of small population genetics is still largely theoretical. "We know inbreeding's bad if you're a human," he says, "but the deleterious effects for wild populations are very controversial. It's not at all clear whether inbreeding is as much of a problem for some wild populations. And some vertebrates, like Japa-nese quail and wolves, regularly inbreed." Peterson says there seems to be an optimum level of inbreeding for each species. For some, inbreeding can allow quick adaptation to change. That's a great benefit in a harsh environment.

The highly organized structure of a wolf pack typically in-cludes only one breeding male and female, called the "alpha pair." This structure ensures a genetic bottleneck. The worst-case scenario is this: as Peterson flies over his natural labora-tory this winter, the wolves he sees, and every wolf born in Isle Royale since the colony was founded, may carry the genetic inheritance of just one pair of wolves.

Peterson's brief time with the four tranquilized wolves included a quick look into their mouths. Their teeth indicated that none of these wolves was past middle age, that is, two to six years old. The females, especially, looked young, perhaps even too young to mate. At least genetic problems, if there are any, have not led to total reproductive failure.

In a larger territory, as the pack expands, individuals break away to form their own packs, thus enlarging the gene pool. At Isle Royale, the only new gene mix occurs when one of the alpha wolves dies.

Because the Isle Royale wolf population is probably the best-known in existence, its disappearance due to inbreeding would be an "instructive extinction." Peterson says: "There would be value in monitoring it to its logical outcome because it will serve as a test case for small-population viability in the face of genetic problems. It's a really tangible example of what's going to happen all through the world."

Dr. Robert Wayne's laboratory at UCLA is not evocative of high technology, nor of ample funds. The desks are battered and the basement-level rooms are hospital green. Tiers of olive-drab cabinets store a collection of fossilized bones from the dinosaur period.

Wayne's business, however, is with species that are not extinct, not quite. With techniques developed only in the last few years, he can analyze the genetic "fingerprints" of individual animals to see how closely they are related. He can discern genetic differences between groups of, say, Channel Island kit foxes, and recommend whether they should be protected as distinct subspecies. And he can tell a zoo in Nairobi whether its specimen is a side-striped jackal or the progeny of a domestic dog and a black-backed jackal.

One recent afternoon, Wayne took delivery of an ordinary-looking cardboard parcel and split it open, removing vials of dark, chilled wolf blood. The samples were centrifuged and set aside in a refrigerator with others from Isle Royale and from Voyageurs National Park and Superior National Forest, both in

Minnesota. More wolf-blood samples are expected from Denali and Gates of the Arctic national parks in Alaska, and from Vancouver Island, Manitoba, and northern Ontario.

Wayne's first task will be to answer some questions about the four Isle Royale wolves. Is there much variability in their genetic inheritance? How closely related are they? Have grandparents mated with grandchildren? Sibling with sibling? Then come comparisons with other, larger wolf populations. How much genetic variability do they show? How much is characteristic of the species? Which population is most closely related to the Isle Royale group?

Deciphering the signs of variation or uniformity encrypted along those famous double helixes takes several weeks of shrewd, patient work. DNA strings are made up of thousands of pairs of coded proteins, one-half of each pair inherited from each of the parents. Certain enzymes can be mixed in with the DNA, and these enzymes are able to recognize the chemical pattern of specific pairs. The enzyme performs a useful trick: when it hits that pattern, it makes a cut in the DNA.

After treatment with twenty different enzymes, the chopped-up strings of DNA from different wolves can be compared. The more closely the segments match, the more closely related the wolves are. By this spring, Wayne's tests should be near completion. The National Park Service is an atypical client, he says. It is paying for the job. Most of his work on behalf of exotic and fast-disappearing vertebrates is not funded, and he has to do it on the side.

The government and foundation sources that academics usually turn to are not eager to finance these investigations, because they are viewed as applied, rather than theoretical, research. Industry, often the financial engine for applied research at universities, has no current interest in the genetics of endangered species, either.

Wayne is part of an upstart and ill-defined field called conservation biology, which has risen from scientific concern for threatened species. One of the field's preoccupations is "minimum viable populations" (MVP)—the number of animals necessary to ensure a given species' survival. The gene pool is only one facet of that problem.

Other MVP issues include:

- How long do we want to plan for a species to endure? Ten years, ten thousand?
- At what level of certainty do we want to try to guarantee a species' survival: 75 percent, 100?
- Is it better to establish one large preserve or several smaller ones? A large one offers more isolation from outside effects. On the other hand, greater numbers of preserves help limit catastrophe, say, disease or climate change, by containing the risk.

Since these questions don't arise in a political or an economic vacuum, we can all too easily imagine a range of Solomonic choices. Say there is will and funding enough to prolong the survival of either the snow leopard or the panda at an 80 percent level of certainty. If the resources are divided among the two, they will both become extinct. What's the best decision?

"The world faces an impending crisis of species extinctions," writes the U.S. Fish and Wildlife Service's Mark Shaffer in *Viable Populations for Conservation*. Species extinction "could rank as one of the major biological perturbations in Earth's history."

Even without famine, disease, or inbreeding depression, the wolves of Isle Royale are so few that they could all perish, just with a slight rise of the death rate over the birth rate. Peterson and Tom Drummer, a mathematician also at Michigan Technical University, used a modified version of an MVP model to project the Isle Royale wolf population's viability. From the model they concluded that a population of a dozen wolves faces a one-in-three chance of extinction during the next century. If their number drops to ten, the wolves have only a 50 to 65 percent chance of survival.

"We create wolves," Barry Lopez writes in *Of Wolves and Men*. "The methodology of science creates a wolf just as surely as does the metaphysical vision of a native American." There have been "at different times in history, different places for the wolf to fit; and, at the same moment in history, different ideas of the wolf's place in the universe have existed side by side, even in the same culture."

The wolf's current place in the conservationists' universe as a rare species needing protection seems clear. But wolves also symbolize our sometimes catastrophic interference with natural processes such as predator-prey interaction. The two ideas are deceptively similar. For policy-making purposes, they can be flatly at odds.

Although Isle Royale is part of the State of Michigan, it is much closer—ecologically and geographically—to Minnesota. Wolves are not an endangered species in Minnesota. "The [U.S. Fish and Wildlife Service] recovery plans for the eastern timber wolf, a new draft of which just came out, say that we should continue to protect the population," Krumenaker says. "But they haven't even dealt with the idea of what to do if it starts to decline. It's something nobody ever anticipated. Then you run up against Park Service policy, which does not say you have to keep your hands off all native populations. What it does say is that, whenever possible, we want all natural ecological processes to continue unimpeded."

Officially, the National Park Service tries to occupy an uncomfortable and shifting middle ground. Human-caused problems, such as a parvo epidemic, tend to justify intervention. If the wolves are threatened by inbreeding or food availability, these "natural" causes argue against intervention. Think of a virus as "unnatural" and you sense the dilemma.

"Where is our best management strategy in terms of preserving what we can of the natural processes?" Krumenaker asks. "Everybody's going to call that a little bit differently." The wolves, after all, only appeared forty years ago. Maybe the island is more natural, not less, without them. It could be argued that the arrival of moose on the island wasn't natural because it was stimulated by settlement on the mainland in the nineteenth century. Eradicating all the moose to turn back the clock would thus be a logical, though extreme, plan. "Maybe the real logical extreme," Krumenaker says, "is to bring back the glaciers."

Much of Wayne's work on the genetics of wolf populations in the region sets the stage for another logic to operate: If all of the island's current wolves died, a whole new pack could be introduced. Would Peterson favor such a move? "Based on what I know now, and the philosophical perspective I come from, yes," he says. But the National Park Service, he believes, is "nowhere near" making such a decision.

Krumenaker, observing that the decision isn't his to make in any case, says reintroduction is a "conceivable alternative," but there are other views to consider. One was articulated by a Duluth, Minnesota, resident, who wrote to the editor of her local newspaper: "I am thoroughly convinced that nature is wiser than we are in such matters. Often well-intentioned repopulation efforts cause more harm than good because there are so many variables. . . . Nature's balancing process takes time and trust, and does not always work out as we'd like. . . . Wolves are just one chapter in Isle Royale's rich history. Don't edit the book before it's finished."

Krumenaker and others in the National Park Service hold out some hope for having it both ways. "One of the things I think we have to look at in debating whether or not to reintroduce wolves, if they declined to zero, would be the condition of the wolf population in Ontario right now," he says.

"I would argue that that's really important to a decision whether to introduce or not. Is the likelihood of natural immigration the same as it was forty years ago or is it less? Maybe it's greater. We just don't know."

Peterson is skeptical that another trip across the ice could occur. The growth of population centers on the Ontario shore-line opposite Isle Royale presents a new barrier to migration. "Even if it was possible, I think you will have to ask whether that is the most proper use for that island. Is it really so impor-tant, philosophically, to allow natural colonization that we'd sit back and suffer through what is going to be an ecological nightmare when those moose cut loose? What we would see is a repeat of the 1930s, which was a disaster," Peterson warns.

As recent controversies over California condors and Yellow-stone grizzlies have shown, however, mistrust of the judgments of both science and wildlife managers runs deep. "In Africa I've run into trouble," Wayne says, "with people who believe a hands-off attitude is important. Don't touch the animals! The Cape hunting dog, for instance. The most endangered carni-vore in all of East Africa. There are only two hundred of them left. No one's doing anything about them." Wayne has not even been permitted to handle these wolflike animals to check for the effects of inbreeding.

"We should get in there and do something," Wayne says. "I think people don't realize that we manipulate everything else. We're responsible for many things in nature. We should be responsible for endangered species in the same way, because we're manipulating them indirectly. We're destroying their habitat. We're destroying their prey base."

It's cold at Isle Royale National Park this winter (1989), but who knows? Two years ago the winter weather was odd, with high temperatures and the thinnest snow cover in twenty years. Last April, Peterson worried about the unseasonable heat. The four wolves did well during and after their brief cap-tivity, but they could not pant while tranquilized. "They were wearing a winter coat. We were wearing shorts," he said. "So they all got hot and thirsty."

This past year—the first noticeable year of the ozone hole and, perhaps, the greenhouse effect—summer came early. It was the hottest anyone could remember. At the west end of the island single tracks were seen, but no sign of a wolf pack. And for the first summer in a long, long while, no howls were heard.

Eighteen years later, Rolf Peterson said that the region seems to have significantly warmer winters. "In the last ten years, we have found ice insufficient for normal operation twice when we started our winter study, and once we have been melted out in February and forced to leave early."

The wolf population stayed low into the mid-1990s, and has been slowly increasing since, to a high of thirty. "They're doing very, very well for the moment," he said.

Parvovirus was determined by lab work to be the most likely cause of their sharp decline during the 1980s, though genetics may have been a contributing factor. And by chance, Peterson discovered that a dog had died of parvo in Duluth in 1981, a few days after illegally visiting Isle Royale, when it would have been "hot"—shedding viruses. It had contracted parvo from another ailing dog visiting from Chicago. The unprecedented wolf pup die-off started soon after.

After thirty-five years of study, he has concluded that "unpredictability is the hallmark of this system. The longer the studies go on, the more we are aware of the extent of our ignorance, which is profound. Rare, unpredictable events can change everything. Everything we're seeing now in wolf-moose dynamics is traceable to the dog from Chicago in July 1981."

The Songbird Connection

Spring Creek emerges quietly from some generous subterranean source, in a pond on the margins of Minnesota's St. Croix River Valley. Then the water picks up speed as it tumbles over an old dam, and you begin to hear it. A pleasant sound, perhaps, but disturbing for research zoologist Richard Weisbrod. So is the lilting clarity of the occasional birdsong.

"I was raised in this part of the world," he says. "Twenty years ago, you couldn't distinguish a Baltimore oriole from an ovenbird. It was a cacophony of avian vocalizations. Now, at midmorning in the middle of May, you can even hear the stream. And there are no thrushes. There ought to be all sorts of thrushes here."

The dozens of bird species that migrate to or through the St. Croix National Scenic Riverway from Latin America each spring should be thriving. Part of the national park system, the corridor offers 252 miles of protected habitat.

But Weisbrod's lament is not just misplaced nostalgia. Reports of the decline or disappearance of migratory bird populations have been accumulating from widely scattered areas across the country. The phenomenon is not restricted to shore and wetland species and majestic birds of prey, many of them recognized as rare or threatened for decades. Now the species reported as scarce or missing from areas where they were formerly abundant are songbirds, familiar even to the casual backyard observer: orioles, tanagers, warblers, flycatchers, redstarts.

Several factors have made scientists cautious about sounding an alarm, however, and some still call the evidence inconclusive. For one thing, bird populations can change dramatically from year to year, even under normal conditions. Without reliable, continuous data collected over many years—twenty years is an accepted minimum—who could say whether the reported declines were within the realm of natural variation?

But new research has led to a growing scientific consensus: population declines among many migratory species are real, abnormal, severe, and widespread.

At a recent symposium, Clemson University ornithologist Sidney Gauthreaux reported on his preliminary comparison of radar images of the massive bird migrations across the Gulf of Mexico. The numbers staggered some of his colleagues: the density of the flocks had dropped by half over the past twenty years.

A recent analysis of data collected in the North American Breeding Bird Survey (BBS) shows sharp declines among a score of migrant land bird species. But to talk about extinctions in these species is premature, according to U.S. Fish and Wildlife Service ornithologist Sam Droege, one of the study's authors. "The gist of our paper is to say, 'Watch out—where will the bottom line be? We don't know where the situation will end.'"

Droege and his coauthors say their data strongly implicate the rapid deforestation of Mexico and Central and South America—crucial habitat for many migrants. Other scientists argue that forest fragmentation in our own country is a more significant factor in the declines, partly because some birds will breed only in deep forests. Fragmented woods also afford far less protection from predators and from parasitic birds that prefer forest edges.

Before proposing action, scientists would prefer to sort out the relative importance of these environmental changes and track population shifts among a long list of migrant species, especially those most threatened. That process is still in its infancy, however, and time may be short. The BBS, so far the best source of data, is "wide, but shallow," says Purdue ecologist Kerry Rabenold. It consists of bird counts made by volunteers who have driven more than two thousand different prescribed routes around the United States and Canada each summer since 1966.

"I distrust its ability to detect declines in species we're most concerned about," he says. "It's a roadside survey, so it wouldn't get at deep-forest species, which are in the greatest peril. And the survey can't cope, statistically, with the low numbers of rarer species to see how bad the declines really are."

At Great Smoky Mountains National Park, Rabenold and a team of students rolled out of bed at 4:30 a.m. each day during the breeding season to cross-check the accuracy of the BBS with other techniques and to look for ways that it might be modified for use in the park system. They are part of a grass-roots effort called the Migratory Bird Watch, slowly growing within the Park Service, whose organizers hope to build an international monitoring and conservation network. Administrators in each park have been invited to set up the essential long-term bird counts and to establish symbolic "linkages" with other parks to focus attention on the migrants.

The linkages are an interpretive device to remind park visitors of the interdependence of the hemisphere's natural preserves. Blackpoll warblers and eastern wood-pewees, for example, breed in Acadia National Park, Maine, and pass through the Everglades during their migratory cycles. The olive-sided fly-catcher and Townsend's warbler link Mount Rainier in Washington and Arizona's Chiricahua National Monument, which they pass through on their way south for the winter. For the long-distance migrants, of course, these connections extend on southward, to the rest of the hemisphere.

"I think the key is raising awareness among the American public that protecting and preserving those birds, which we take for granted, is dependent on international cooperation," says Richard Cunningham, chief interpreter for the Park Service's western region.

So far, administrators at about a dozen national parks have incorporated the Migratory Bird Watch into their research and interpretive programs. But a proposal to extend it to all suitable national park areas, and an initiative to foster cooperative efforts in Latin American countries, has attracted scant support among decision makers in the upper echelons of the park system.

Though their land mass is too tiny to afford real protection, the national parks have a crucial role to play in the future, bird research scientists say. The parks provide a baseline for comparison with other, less protected areas, essential in attempts to explain what is happening to the migrants. Yet today very little is known about the size and health of bird populations in our national parks. "The Fish and Wildlife Service is getting religion about doing that kind of basic monitoring," Rabenold says, "and the Park Service is, too, to a lesser degree."

About half the birds in the national parks are long-distance migrants. Of some 650 bird species that breed in North America, Cunningham points out, 332 migrate beyond the boundaries of the United States. Though we may think of them as "our birds," they spend two-thirds of their lives on the migratory journey and on their southern wintering grounds. Migration routes can stretch thousands of miles, from Amazonia to the Arctic, but the largest numbers of birds winter in Central America and the Caribbean islands.

The wood thrush, for example, inhabits lowland rainforests from southern Mexico to Panama during the winter season. Its breeding range extends roughly across the eastern half of the United States. Robin-sized, feathered mostly in shades of brown, the wood thrush is not one of the more eye-catching migrants, but its song is among the sweetest. "Whenever a man hears it, he is young, and Nature is in her spring," Thoreau wrote. "Wherever he hears it, it is a new world and a free country, and the gates of heaven are not shut against him."

Wood thrush populations are falling fast, according to the BBS study (see table at the end of this chapter).

Smithsonian biologist John Rappole sees thrushes during spring and summer research in Virginia's Shenandoah National Park, and, during the winter, in Mexico's Tuxtla Mountains Biosphere Preserve. That nobly named area, however, is a preserve only on paper. "We started work there in 1973," he says. "Since that time the amount of forest has declined from 30 percent to 15 percent, replaced by pasture. There are no wood thrushes in pasture areas."

Population pressure in Mexico and throughout Latin America drives subsistence farmers farther and farther into the rainforest, where they log areas unsuited for farming. "You're talking about slopes of 45 degrees, rainfall of 160 inches a year. They get two years of use out of a field. There isn't much forest left. At some point they're going to run out, and they're still going to be facing the same problems. It's a situation that can't go on." Furthermore, once cleared, rainforests do not regenerate. Estimates of the rate of destruction of tropical forests throughout Latin America range from 1 to 3.5 percent per year and possibly higher.

Neither is the wood thrush's summer habitat, north of the border, secure against threats. Cowbird populations have reportedly swollen in many areas, including the Rocky Mountains, where larger forests have been split up into smaller patches. An edge-dwelling parasite, the cowbird lays eggs in the nests of other species, sometimes destroying the eggs of the host bird. Any survivors face tough competition, as the big cowbird chicks usually hatch earlier, grow faster, and eat more of the food provided by their "adoptive" parents.

In the fragmented woods around Lake Shelbyville, Illinois, an important regional breeding area for songbirds, one recent study found that cowbirds had parasitized 80 percent of the nests of all other species. In wood thrush nests, cowbird eggs outnumbered thrush eggs four to one. The thrushes were doing little but raising cowbirds, researcher Scott Robinson found.

National parks afford more protection, but Rappole's research shows how park management practices can alter the balance of survival for any species. Songbirds like the wood thrush, for example, breed in just the kind of greenery that is eaten by deer. In Shenandoah and many other national parks, Rappole says, deer populations are now about ten times their natural density. The timber wolves and mountain lions that kept deer populations in check before human settlement have not been reintroduced. "The deer just clean out the understory," he says. "It looks, from the ground level to four feet, like somebody's gone through with clippers."

To avoid predators or starvation, long-distance migrants depend on healthy ecosystems in two places, usually thousands of miles apart. But to call their situation "double jeopardy" leaves out the real drama of their survival.

"The experience that has moved me more than anything else," says Ted Simons, research biologist at Gulf Islands National Seashore, "has been watching these birds appear after they have flown fifteen to twenty-four hours or more, nonstop, across the Gulf. They weigh only eight to twelve grams, and they have flown five or six hundred miles."

Some stumble aimlessly, so tired they are willing even to be picked up in human hands, he said. They are vivid against the white sand of the barrier islands, like hopping Christmas lights. "It's really spectacular to see these brightly colored birds—indigo buntings and blackburnian warblers, scarlet tanagers, yellow warblers—foraging, trying to build up their energy supply so they can continue migrating."

The birds stay from a couple of hours to a couple of weeks. Moving to the island's north side, they flutter uncertainly, as if making up their minds to leave. Then, airborne, they head north at thirty miles an hour or so, up along the Mississippi toward the St. Croix River country, perhaps, or northeast to the Smokies, the Appalachians, or Canada.

"The period of migration, just from a survival standpoint, is very critical and very stressful, especially for the trans-Gulf migrants," Simons explains. "They have very little latitude, at that point, to continue or keep looking for suitable habitat. If they don't find it, they're in big trouble. They don't have the luxury to go on another couple of hundred miles."

There are only guesses as to how quickly stopover habitat may be disappearing within or south of our national borders, but few doubt that it is. The river forests of Texas are an important flyway, for instance, and they are falling fast, Rappole says.

"And just like musical chairs," a Gulf Island migration report notes, "there aren't enough places to go around. . . . Remove this habitat and we pull an irreplaceable chair out from under millions of migrating birds whose stake in the game is survival."

Richard Weisbrod is now retired and living on San Juan Island in Washington state, where, he reports, the human population has quintupled in ten years and bird populations are, predictably, declining.

John Rappole, who still works at the Smithsonian research facility, says the decline of wood thrush habitat in the Tuxtla preserve has continued, along with deforestation throughout Latin America, at the same pace. Deer populations, and their appetites, remain high at Shenandoah National Park. Wood thrush populations have continued their steady decline.

The U.S. Fish and Wildlife Service's national annual Breeding Bird Survey charts trends in bird populations. Below are the latest data available as of this writing, showing the trend for the twenty most quickly declining species, including the wood thrush, during the survey's existence so far. Keith Pardieck, BBS coordinator, has also calculated for this table the effects on their populations so far, and if the declines continue at the same rate during the coming century. Only the species for which statistical confidence levels are high were included.

Species	Trend estimate 1966–2004 (%/yr)	Overall population change 1966–2004	Projected population change (%) 1966–2050	Projected population change (%) 1966–2100
Cerulean warbler	–3.8	–77.4	–96.3	–99.5
Baird's sparrow	–3.8	–76.7	–96.0	–99.4
Grasshopper sparrow	–3.5	–74.6	–95.2	–99.2
Olive-sided flycatcher	–3.3	–72.5	–94.2	–98.9
Golden-winged warbler	–3.0	–68.0	–91.9	–98.2
Brewer's sparrow	–2.6	–62.6	–88.6	–96.9
Lark sparrow	–2.4	–60.7	–87.3	–96.3
Bell's vireo	–2.3	–58.8	–85.9	–95.6
Black-billed cuckoo	–2.2	–56.5	–84.1	–94.7
Whip-poor-will	–2.2	–56.3	–83.9	–94.6
Mountain plover	–2.1	–56.1	–83.8	–94.5
Prairie warbler	–2.1	–54.7	–82.6	–93.9
Rufous hummingbird	–1.8	–50.5	–78.9	–91.6
Painted bunting	–1.8	–49.1	–77.5	–90.7
Yellow-billed cuckoo	–1.7	–48.5	–76.9	–90.3
Chuck-will's-widow	–1.7	–47.1	–75.5	–89.4
Wood thrush	–1.6	–46.8	–75.2	–89.2
Eastern wood-pewee	–1.6	–45.4	–73.8	–88.2
Chimney swift	–1.5	–44.7	–73.0	–87.6
Canada warbler	–1.5	–43.7	–71.9	–86.8

Mallows,
Marking Time

 The Peter's Mountain mallow, Virginia's rarest plant and one of the rarest in the nation, is having a difficult summer.

The last three wild plants known to exist anywhere are three feet tall and apparently healthy, growing high on a ridge in Giles County. But two years of severe drought and an unexplained ailment have caused nearly all of the plants' quarter-sized pink flowers to abort before producing new seeds.

"We were very disappointed," said Tom Wieboldt, assistant curator of the herbarium at Virginia Polytechnic Institute and State University. "It looked like we were going to get a lot of seed from the plants in the wild." He is still confident of the plant's ultimate survival. It is a perennial, and it can send up new sprouts from its roots as well as from seeds. But the new problem, perhaps genetic in origin, has weakened an important defense against extinction. "We're down to so few individuals that it's certainly one of the rarest plants in the United States," said Richard Dyer, an endangered species biologist with the federal Fish and Wildlife Service. "None in the Northeast or the Southeast are in as dire straits. Any chance event, a fire or some other catastrophe, could effectively eliminate them."

Dyer's office provides 90 percent of the $4,000 budgeted to protect the mallow during this fiscal year and the state, 10 percent. Some of the funds go to Virginia Tech graduate student John Randall, who climbs Peter's Mountain each week to check on the plants, stepping around occasional copperheads and timber rattlers. On his visits, he lugs a string of gallon water jugs up the steep trail to allay the drought, and he has helped fashion chicken-wire enclosures to keep out deer, which have a keen appetite for the mallows. Last fall someone chanced on the site, pulled down the enclosures, and yanked one of the stems out of the ground, but it survived a replanting.

Wieboldt and Randall gathered all the 1/8-inch, kidney-shaped seeds they could find near the mallows last year, and gleaned more during hours of sifting through leaf litter brought down from the mountain. A dozen of the total of about 120 they collected were planted. Five plants grow in a garden in Wieboldt's house, seven at Randall's, but they have not yet borne seeds—another disappointment, Wieboldt said.

Marshall Trammell, supervisor of the state bureau charged with plant protection, acknowledges that the importance of a few mallows nearing extinction on a remote mountain ridge may not be readily apparent. "The same questions have been asked ever since the word 'endangered' has come into use: Why do anything? Why not let it pass by, as the dinosaurs did?" The answers, he said, "are never going to please everybody." Many pharmaceutical products are derived from plants, and rare species can also answer scientific questions about how plants and animals function, sometimes serving as an environmental early-warning system. "Whether it's an esoteric value or actual, practical, down-to-earth value that can be applied today, the problem is, once an entity is extinct, you lose any ability to assess any of its potential."

Wieboldt advanced another argument: "We may never get anything worthwhile from this plant, but I think we have a real need to show concern for things that are disappearing around us. I think that if you take the attitude that these things aren't that important, then where do you draw the line? You can just let your whole environment go down the tubes. And somewhere you've got to decide that things are worthwhile, worth saving, worth preserving."

Research is part of the mallow preservation effort, to add to the little that is known about its habitat, its biology, and the reasons for its decline. Near the top of the list of questions is the unexpected and perplexing failure to produce seeds. In addition to research, Wieboldt will check other mountain areas determined to have the right combinations of altitude, soil, sun, and rainfall, on the outside chance he will find more of the plants.

"All of the possibilities have not been exhausted yet, that's for sure," he said. But other researchers have checked many similar locales without success since the first and only colony was identified in 1927. Several hundred mallows were counted then, but some that looked separate may have sprung instead from the roots of a single parent. "One of the big questions in everyone's mind is whether people have been counting the same thing over the years," Wieboldt said.

The plant's history seems vexed by such complexities. Botanists disagreed until a few years ago on whether the Peter's Mountain mallow was the same species as its nearest relative, the Kankakee mallow, a mostly midwestern river-bottom dweller that is also quite rare. Government agencies assign plants of doubtful pedigree a lower priority for protection.

Then an Ohio researcher planted seeds from both types. His observations established a scientific consensus that they were, indeed, distinct species, Wieboldt said. That cleared the way for the Peter's Mountain mallow to be placed, May 12, 1986, on the federal endangered species list.

It is also a candidate for the Virginia list, but state law requires that property owners, adjacent owners, and other interested parties be notified and asked for their response beforehand, Trammell explained.

The human heirs to the mallow's last refuge are numerous and far-flung, however, and some have been hard to locate, he said. The newest owner is the Nature Conservancy, a nonprofit group whose goal is to locate and protect examples of rare plant and animal species worldwide. It purchased a fractional interest in 361 acres that include the mallow site for $15,000 in 1985 and is negotiating for the rest, Conservancy attorney Philip Tabas said.

State listing of the mallow as an endangered species may follow. State law prevents anyone from collecting or selling a listed plant and requires a continuing assessment of potential threats. Meanwhile, the Conservancy has played a major role in devising a protection and management plan for the property.

Trammell said the Virginia round-leaf birch and the small-whorled pogonia are the only plants now listed as "endangered" by the state. American ginseng is listed as "threatened," indicating that it is somewhat more secure, but may become endangered in the future. Fifteen other rare plants are being considered for endangered status by Trammell's office. They were recommended for protection by the Virginia Natural Heritage Program, a two-year, $260,000 project jointly financed by the state and the Nature Conservancy.

The heritage program's staff of five is assembling a computerized catalog of occurrences of Virginia's rare plant and animal species in order to assess which are endangered, extinct, or more common than expected, and to provide a basis for future conservation planning.

The most important discovery about the mallow in the years since this article was first written was that its reproduction had halted for lack of fire. The plant has a particularly tough seed coat, according to Tom Wieboldt, and periodic, low-intensity fires are needed to weaken it and allow moisture to enter as a sort of catalyst for germination.

When fire was applied, he said, "There was tremendous response from the seed banks there on Peter's Mountain." Sixty to eighty plants are now scattered along the crest of the ridge, and they have survived more drought years without hand-watering. Two botanical gardens have been supplied with the now-abundant seeds to establish off-site plantings as a hedge against extinction of the species.

Desperately Seeking
Charisma

Maybe your Uncle Lester, a determined foe of garden pests, likes to tease about starting a "save the earwigs" campaign. Or a winking colleague proposes a new pressure group, People for the Ethical Treatment of Insects—the acronym is pronounced "petty."

Invertebrate conservation biology is a subject made to order for gibes. *Homo sapiens* is for the most part a vertebrocentric species, prejudging the spineless classes as near-invisible and boring at best, and as ugly, small, mean, indestructible, over-fecund disease vectors at worst.

"I wish I had a dime for every time someone has asked me why we should care about an insect," says Ming Lee Prospero, a wildlife biologist who breeds dozens of endangered American burying beetles at the Roger Williams Park Zoo in Rhode Island, for a reintroduction project on Nantucket.

The animals are pretty cool—or would be, with the right public relations campaign. A mated pair of the striking red, orange, and black, 1.5-inch carrion beetles can tug a fresh carcass of, say, a mourning dove several feet, completely bury it to keep it away from competitors, strip it of feathers and skin, and then use the burial chamber as a food source and incubator.

The reintroduction experiment, supervised by the U.S. Fish and Wildlife Service, is now in its tenth year, but whether it has been successful in establishing a self-sustaining population of burying beetles is still unknown. Once common across eastern North America, the beetle is now found only in small numbers, in a handful of places.

The reasons for the speed and extent of its disappearance are still largely a mystery, but the burying beetle is emblematic of many other vanishing invertebrates. There are examples in any state. Mountain Virginia, for example, is the last redoubt of a many-legged black-and-yellow detritus-eater called the Laurel Creek millipede, which has been around for 2 or 3 million years. Now, in what has probably been a long diminuendo, it's only known to exist in a single small population, in a sandy streamside rhododendron thicket near an old gristmill on the Blue Ridge Parkway. A fairly extensive search has turned up no others, so this population may be unique. "We know that species go extinct," says entomologist Richard Hoffman, of the Virginia Museum of Natural History, "and in that process, it's got to come down to one last place."

Habitat destruction, invasive aliens, climate change, pesticides, pollution, and perhaps Uncle Lester are taking their toll, in the now-familiar, honey-I-ate-the-planet scenario that makes humankind an urgent "species of interest" for scientists who normally study other organisms.

Zoologist Larry Master of Nature-Serve, a conservation data network, says 20 to 35 percent of known terrestrial invertebrate species in North America are "in some kind of conservation jeopardy." For example, half of the species of terrestrial snails, one-fifth of butterflies and skippers, a quarter of 104 kinds of tiger beetles, a third of grasshoppers, 18 percent of moths, and 90 percent of cave-dwelling organisms are vulnerable to extinction. "Groups that are the subject of much popular public and media attention, such as birds and mammals, are proportionately and numerically much less at risk," Master says.

Princeton zoologist Claire Kremen points out that invertebrates are almost unimaginably diverse. Insects alone make up more than half of the planet's 1.75 million or so described species. Of the 8 million or more different species that may exist undescribed, 80 percent are probably insects. In an Amazon rainforest ecosystem, invertebrates account for an estimated 90 percent of the animal biomass, and they probably number in the billions, compared to mere hundreds or thousands of birds and mammals.

Invertebrate specialists insist that it is not only the so-called keystone species at the top of the food chain that hold up the arch of the biome but also the tiny organisms that crawl around in the dirt under the whole structure—the little things that run the world, in E. O. Wilson's phrase.

The ecosystem services that invertebrates supply are no less crucial because they go unappreciated. Some are decomposers—those earwigs and millipedes—recycling waste organic matter and aerating, building, and blending soils. Invertebrate herbivores shape the ecology and evolution of plants. Predator species control and help stabilize the populations of the animal organisms they feed on.

Kremen's lab group has studied the role of insects as pollinators in California melon fields. The researchers found that fields adjacent to natural areas, and farms where pesticide use is curtailed, sustain a far broader mix of pollinator species, in much higher numbers. This could save farmers the expense of importing honeybees to their fields and result in higher melon production.

Getting that kind of story in front of food producers and the public at large is crucial, Kremen says, now that more invertebrate researchers must think of themselves as conservation biologists. "What's crucial is for people to understand how important these organisms are to our own survival," she adds. "For pollination, we're relying entirely on one species, the honeybee. But the domesticated colonies have declined by 50 percent in the last fifty years. What if they keep declining? If we also fail to care for the other wild pollinators, by using pesticides and destroying their habitat, we may be out of luck one day on food production and . . . other services that are less well studied."

At a recent symposium at New York's American Museum

of Natural History, characterized by one of its organizers as a "coming-out party" for invertebrate conservation biology, several speakers noted that agriculture, properly adapted, can serve as a repository for invertebrate diversity rather than a near-sterile wasteland.

Politics was also on the agenda. Scripps Institution oceanographer Jeremy Jackson warned that "science-as-usual" cannot meet the challenge of our ecologically disrupted oceans. They are quickly losing habitat-structuring species—including invertebrate animals such as coral—to ruinous climate change, pollution, bottom-scraping trawlers, dynamiting, and over-fishing, he said.

Jackson is working with filmmakers in California to try to reach a public "that thinks *USA Today* is an intellectual publication," with simple, direct messages. He urged his colleagues to "wade in . . . and say what we think. And we'll be wrong some percentage of the time, and we are really afraid to do that. So I think a big component of courage would be a major contribution."

Public education also takes more lighthearted forms, such as the Insect Fear Film Festival, now in its twenty-first year of screening old bug-monster movies to large audiences, with a full complement of media coverage, T-shirts, and invertebrate reality checks as a counterweight to the cinema stereotypes. The audience is invited to see and handle a variety of live specimens—a "meet the stars" opportunity—such as tarantulas, hissing cockroaches, and tobacco hornworms. On occasion, deep-fried waxworms, stir-fried silkworm pupae, and lollipops with maguey worms are served. The University of Illinois event was initiated by May Berenbaum, now head of the Department of Entomology. For more tender ages, coloring books and grade-school curricula can bring the fascination of invertebrates into focus.

"We haven't gotten the story out to the public about the indispensability of invertebrates," said Sacha Spector, director of the museum's invertebrate conservation program.

"One of the things I like most is getting kids to look at them under a microscope. Because once they do, an entire new world is opened up for them—eyes and legs and a mouth—and it stops being this speck that's easily stepped on." Advances in technology also hold some promise. Instead of exchanging specimen organisms through the mails for study and identification, for example—a slow, expensive, and damage-prone tradition—high-resolution images and data are now increasingly available on the Internet.

Thousands of katydids and bush crickets are on view along with complete descriptions and even some sound files, for example, at www.tettigonia.com. Type "Paraguay" in the distribution box and records for forty-two taxa appear, including hyperdetailed images of the wing and head of *Caulopsis oberthuri*, which would doubtless have been tough for researchers to arrange to get a look at in earlier times.

At another Web site, more than twenty-eight thousand species from the entomology collection of the Museum of Comparative Zoology at Harvard University—one of the largest in North America—are on offer. For science, these innovations may help reduce the dimensions of the "black hole" of ignorance about invertebrates, only a small fraction of which have been described, let alone comprehended in detail.

Ironically, a new species of centipede was discovered in Central Park, across the street from the Museum of Natural History, only two years ago. "It tells us something shocking about what we don't know, rather than what we know," museum provost Michael Novacek said at the time.

Biologists will have turned a corner in public education when the citizenry can appreciate the need to protect the tenuous hold on existence of a species like Southern California's Delhi Sands flower-loving fly. Its endangered status thwarted the entrepreneurial plans of a few *Homo sapiens* recently and seemed to galvanize a somewhat sarcastic public mistrust about invertebrate conservation. Land developers brought flyswatters to public meetings. A bullied U.S. Fish and Wildlife Service, charged with developing a conservation plan, worried about squandering its meager fund of public goodwill.

In the meantime, invertebrate conservation biologists may have to coach themselves to stave off depression, an occupational hazard.

"What keeps me going are little rays of hope, here and there," Kremen says. She cites the rise in sales of organic food, which should help the pollinators, and a recent decision by the Madagascar government to extend protection to as much as 10 percent of the nation's land surface.

World per-capita consumption of freshwater has declined, aquatic ecologist David Strayer says, thanks to drip irrigation systems, which "means more to freshwater invertebrates than any invertebrate-based conservation effort I can think of."

And Mace Vaughn, conservation director of the Xerxes Society, the only invertebrate conservation organization in the United States, cites other improvements to cleave to:

The group has recently published a "red list" of some 120 different pollinator insects in need of conservation measures that has gained relatively wide attention. And after years of hard work at both the local and national level, Nebraska's extremely rare Salt Creek tiger beetle was placed in late 2005 on the federal endangered species list.

It was, Vaughn hopes, a bellwether. "More and more land managers, not just at the U.S. Fish and Wildlife Service but at the Bureau of Land Management and the Forest Service, are interested in thinking about ecosystem functions and the role of invertebrates," he said, and the trend has become more evident in just the past couple of years.

Agroterror

Terrorism seems a remote threat at the 1,200-acre Arrowhead Ranch, where Clay Boscamp has run cattle for the past forty years. The nearest urban area is Waelder, Texas, population 947, and the closest thing to a security operation is the local Neighborhood Watch. "I sure don't worry about it much," Boscamp says. "I feel pretty confident the government has made plans."

Instead, the government is scrambling to begin to make some plans just now, though operations such as Boscamp's have not been forgotten. A recent report for the Department of Defense, titled *Hitting America's Soft Underbelly*, says that though it's possible to infest crops with diseases or pests, livestock such as the three hundred head of cattle and twenty-five thousand chickens on the Arrowhead Ranch are a far likelier target.

A virulent disease such as avian influenza or foot-and-mouth, which infects cows, sheep, and pigs, might spread quickly. Gonzales County is thick with cattle, so many that it's on the national top-10 list for potential threats, Boscamp says. And garrisoning miles of fence lines against intruders isn't practical, so early detection and response are crucial. "There's no barrier that you could possibly have [that would] keep someone from throwing something onto your land," he says. "Cattle herds are really unprotected, as far as that kind of threat."

Ironically, a far larger biological threat to American agriculture—alien plants, animals, and diseases we accidentally import that are killing food crops and wild species in natural areas, too—is already well under way, and comparatively unnoticed. Spotted knapweed, soybean rust, Asian long-horned beetles, purple loosestrife, mile-a-minute weed, sudden oak death, and hundreds of other pests are loose on the land or making a strong bid to get here.

News reports usually treat new outbreaks of foreign pests as isolated events—here, an unwelcome new population of snakehead fish in the Potomac watershed; there, zebra mussels over the eastern half of North America; in the Midwest, an explosion of emerald ash borer beetles—rather than a pattern of trouble. Only recently has their combined impact been tabulated, in a study that estimates the annual cost of what's already here at $137 billion, and more than half of that figure is due to losses in the agriculture sector. Take a single state—Virginia, for example. The study's author, Cornell University's David Pimentel, estimates the costs of invasive species in that state alone at $1.5 to $3 billion. Annually.

"And that is one of the challenges," says Jamie Reaser, until recently one of the directors of the federal agency that is trying to coordinate the work of fighting invasive foreign pests. "The people working on this issue, their dance cards are full. It is such a big issue, and at this point in time we need more people, more resources, more dedicated staff to get the job done, because the people who are doing it are maxed out." We'd do well to worry more about self-inflicted biological pollution—a real, not a theoretical, threat like agroterror—Reaser says.

But convincing the public, let alone our national leadership, that our carelessness makes us a biohazard on our own landscape is a tough sale. Other kinds of terrorist threats occupy the national radar screen for now, so the Department of Homeland Security (DHS) has announced the award of $33 million (U.S.) in three-year grants to university-based scientists to study ways to defend against agroterror: deliberate biological attacks on the nation's farms and food processors to spread panic and inflict economic losses.

In the nearer term, new "sniffer" sensor technology that continuously samples the air around livestock or food facilities is one possible countermeasure. Tom McGinn, until recently the emergency programs director for the North Carolina agricultural department and now with the Department of Homeland Security, told a Senate Governmental Affairs Committee hearing last fall that Congress should "develop a national, highly integrated, yet automated, disease detection and surveillance capability."

McGinn envisions "remote, automated radiological, chemical, and biopathogen sensor systems" that could act as a national trip-wire system if it were integrated with GIS (geographic information systems) databases. He calls hand-held biopathogen detection systems "a critical need." The technology is ready, he says, but the government will have to pay to have it produced and activated.

Though some have predicted that the "farm-to-fork infrastructure" will be the next terrorist target, RAND Corporation policy analyst Peter Chalk, author of the *Underbelly* report for the Defense Department, points out that this kind of attack hasn't occurred so far. In the terrorists' cost-benefit calculations, targeting humans may seem more effective for now. Media images of millions of sacrificed animals could suit a terrorist's agenda by spreading fear and dismay, but agroterrorism would not have the drama of a suicide bombing. It's not as media-focused, and publicity is a key objective of terrorist acts.

"Having said that, if you've got a fairly sophisticated group or one that is prepared to think out of the box," Chalk says, "carrying out an attack against the food chain as a secondary form of aggression that is designed to further disorient, destabilize, or panic society—that does have potential credence."

Most of the fifteen "List A" pathogens named by the World Organization of Animal Health can live for extended periods on organic or inorganic matter and are not the targets of current U.S. vaccination campaigns. Several of these disease agents cannot spread to humans, so they would be easy for a terrorist to handle.

The impact of a major U.S. agricultural/food-related disaster would register in several ways, Chalk's report says. First would be economic disruption from direct losses, including the cost of containment and of destroyed animals. Economic ripples through related sectors and the huge cost of trade quarantines imposed against U.S. exports by other countries would quickly add to the bill. U.S. livestock are often bred and reared in extremely crowded conditions, so outbreaks of contagion, especially airborne varieties, are difficult to contain and require the destruction of all exposed livestock, sometimes at great cost. Exotic Newcastle disease in California led to the slaughter of more than 3 million chickens in October 2002.

Large livestock are even more susceptible to disease than chickens because of sterilization, inbreeding, dehorning, branding, hormone injections, and the overuse of antibiotics. The animal disease–reporting system is passive, creating yet another problem. The system relies on individual producers who may have little incentive to be alert and to pass along information, because in many cases they aren't indemnified against losses or quarantines.

Moreover, veterinarians are declining in number, and most want to minister to dogs and cats in the suburbs, where the rewards are highest. Along with new incentives to induce more enrollments in large-animal veterinary programs and better indemnification for farmers, Chalk's recommendations include a comprehensive needs analysis and a prioritizing of agroterror initiatives. Such initiatives are currently "somewhat patchworky," "ad hoc," and "flavor of the day," he says, and scarce resources are misallocated as a result. Funding is "still at the margins, compared with other kinds of homeland security."

Advocates for stepped-up programs say the payoffs for public health and safety from improved protection and inspection measures would be far greater than just short-circuiting agricultural sabotage. The United States is ill-equipped to handle natural or accidental occurrences of disease or contamination of the food supply, which are far more likely and can happen more frequently than a terrorism attack.

"It's only a matter of time before foot-and-mouth disease is imported into this country by natural means," says Mark Wheelis, a University of California, Davis, molecular biologist whose specialty has become bioweapons control policy. "We have to be prepared to respond." Wheelis contends that the government should subsidize a crash vaccine program against the most threatening foreign animal diseases. None exists now. "I think that is a mistake on the part of the government, which is not looking to the long term," he says. "This is an urgent short-term problem, but it is also a chronic problem."

It would be expensive to develop the vaccines and might take ten years, but the losses the country could avoid would be enormous, Wheelis adds. A University of California, Davis, study calculated a minimum cost of a foot-and-mouth outbreak at $13 billion, assuming it was eradicated in just a couple of months and never spread outside California. A national outbreak would scale up accordingly. There is no domestic market for such vaccines except when a disease is introduced, so the government would have to subsidize their development, Wheelis notes.

The DHS and its state-level counterparts aren't likely to pay to put all possible defense strategies to work at Clay Boscamp's ranch, or thousands of others like it. But priorities have to be defined in a far more systematic fashion, Chalk says, with an overall guiding strategy. "At this point, you've just got a bunch of different institutes and a bunch of different initiatives going off in their own directions."

Invasion of the Buggy Snackers (and Other Horrors)

The story line is so familiar, so evocative of old monster movies and *War of the Worlds,* that it's hard to recite in a credible way, even without exclamation points and capital letters: alien species are invading America. And, in the wised-up version of the script, the government seems too conflicted to mount an effective resistance.

A little beyond earshot of the Capitol, for example, in the leafy suburbs of Maryland and Virginia, the chewing sounds may soon be getting loud. Officials in both states are worried that a metallic green Asian beetle that feasts on ash trees may appear in the landscape as it did briefly a few seasons back.

The emerald ash borer probably first arrived at a Great Lakes port in wooden packing material on Korean or Chinese freighters a few years ago. Since then, it has destroyed 6 million trees in Michigan and has also shown up in Ohio and Canada. Ash trees near Wolf Trap in Virginia that might have been infested were cut down recently in an effort to halt any spread of the pest in this area. With luck, it'll work. But if it doesn't, there's a real possibility the borer could do to eastern ash trees what an Asian blight did to chestnuts in the first half of the last century—wipe them out.

Global travel and trade have created a superhighway into the United States for destructive foreign insects, plants, animals, and diseases that scientists call alien invasive species. The long list includes some species that affect humans directly, such as tiger mosquitoes and West Nile virus.

Yet we're pretending we don't have to pay much attention. Countless other destructive alien species are on their way here unless we enact immediate trade policy changes and tougher cargo inspections. The costs will be formidable, but the alternative—more "free trade" in this biological pollution—is far worse.

Bug-watchers in New York and Chicago have a fair idea of how difficult it can be to eradicate new pests in eastern forests. In both those cities a different kind of insect has jumped ship during the past few years. The so-called "Chinese starry sky beetle," aka the Asian long-horned beetle, drills and kills maples and about thirty other kinds of trees. Despite nearly a decade of multiagency quarantines, search-and-destroy missions that have cost tens of millions, and the removal of thousands of urban trees, it's still at large. Yet another Asian beetle with similar broad-gauge appetites has shown up on imported bonsai trees in Washington state.

The problem isn't new, but its scale and frequency are. A 1999 Cornell University study—the most recent attempt to ballpark the price tag—came up with a staggering figure. Damage by species that aren't native to the United States, and the costs of trying to control them, total $137 billion every year. That includes $80 billion in yearly losses for the agriculture sector. (As with all studies, this one from Cornell University is arguable. So just for argument's sake, trim the estimate by a third. You're still looking at a number the size of the annual budget of New York State.)

In Congress, not only the enviro-Democrats are alarmed. Republicans whose League of Conservation Voters' ratings typically hover near zero have also taken aim at infestations in their states.

Idaho's Sen. Larry Craig told the homefolks when he introduced legislation that "We must stop or slow the flow of non-native weeds. . . . Untreated noxious weeds destroy our lands, harm wildlife and native species, and interrupt commerce and recreation for all of those who rely on the land for their livelihoods."

Sen. Ted Stevens of Alaska put in for a $1.5 million appropriation to halt the proliferation of aliens such as the mitten crab and green crab that are threatening fisheries in the North Pacific. Ohio's Rep. George Voinovich introduced legislation to fight water-borne invasives like zebra mussels, silver carp, hydrilla water-weeds, and hundreds of other species in the Great Lakes. "These aquatic terrorists are entering this great natural resource in the ballast water of boats from all over the world, and they must be stopped," Voinovich told a committee hearing. If oratory could kill . . .

Part of the federal anti-invasives effort has been pulled into the Department of Homeland Security because of worry that invasives can be used as a bioterror weapon. Interior Secretary Gail Norton calls the thousands of alien pest species now in the United States "an immense problem" and says eradicating them will require "a tremendous amount of action" by federal and state officials. Mark Rey, the former timber industry lobbyist who now guides national forest policy from the Department of Agriculture, has told a Senate committee that invasives pose an "unusually high threat."

The rhetoric, so far mostly unacted upon, is nonetheless all to the good, because we have a fighting chance against at least some invasives and, especially when new infestations are caught early, successes have been won. After it jumped ship near Wilmington, North Carolina, the Asian gypsy moth was successfully eradicated in the late 1990s in a $3-million campaign. (This species spreads much more quickly than the devastating European gypsy moth we are already stuck with, which feeds on hardwoods. The new one munches conifers, too.)

If you squint hard enough, you can make out another hopeful signal: as pathetically porous as our current border screening system is, it still intercepts an estimated fifty thousand quarantined pests—including several other tries by the Asian gypsy moth—each year. If we put more into the effort, we can keep more pests out.

By all accounts, we are bringing in more new ones all the

time, sometimes accidentally, sometimes on purpose, always carelessly. Most die off soon after they arrive, but some make opportunistic use of this new paradise, which has none of the natural predators that keep their numbers in check in their native habitat.

Congressional and agency initiatives tackle one invader after another, but the most effective and cost-efficient fight can't be waged after the pests are already on the loose. Instead, we need to block the pathways they use to get in.

Broadly speaking, there are two streams of invasive species. One is imported plants and animals for the exotic pet or food trades, and microcritters in dumped ballast water. These are the beneficiaries of laissez-faire regulations that allow them legal entry. The other arrivistes are "stowaway" organisms that slip in inadvertently, on or inside trade goods or packing materials.

It may seem surprising that we haven't heard more about invasives before now. But we really have been, all our lives: kudzu and gypsy moths, killer bees, Japanese beetles and fire ants, chestnut blight and elm disease. Most of those examples are familiar enough that we tend to dismiss them as being safely in the past, something we've gotten used to.

News reports usually treat new problems with invasives as isolated events, rather than a pattern of trouble. It's something like the apocryphal boiling frog experiment. Throw a frog into a tub of hot water and it'll jump out instantly and save itself. But if you start with lukewarm water and heat it gradually, the frog will just swim around until it boils to death.

So, what are we doing about invasives? Federal agencies such as the Department of Agriculture and the Fish and Wildlife Service maintain "dirty lists" that are supposed to keep unwanted organisms out. But among biologists, these lists are little more than a dirty joke because they are laughably incomplete. Remember the snakehead fish that rattled Marylanders when they showed up in a pond a few summers ago? They're 3.5 feet long, aggressive, saw-toothed predators that feed on amphibians, fish, aquatic birds, and small mammals. They can walk on land and survive for days out of water, and they breed like champs.

Snakeheads weren't on the federal "dirty" lists at the time. They were completely legal to import in most states, too, though scientists had warned as early as thirty years before that snakeheads should be banned. Now they finally have been. But now they are at large, reproducing in the Potomac River watershed, and as far as anyone knows, they're unstoppable.

You can still import countless other kinds of potentially destructive fish, killer plants, and exotic animals, such as the Asian swamp eel, a species that is bedeviling Florida's waterways and could easily spread all over the country. I saw a potted tamarisk tree, whose ancestry is Eurasian, for sale outside a grocery store just this week. Tamarisks have sucked watercourses dry and poisoned the trees and soils around them over something like a million acres of riparian wetlands in the western United States, and they are spreading fast.

The National Invasive Species Council (NISC), an interagency group created by executive order in the waning days of the Clinton administration, is trying to orchestrate federal efforts, but with a minuscule staff and a budget to match, it's overburdened.

Indeed, science and management resources across the country are strained. Jamie Reaser, NISC's former international affairs specialist, says, "There is so much happening on this issue right now that it has become a very difficult thing to try to get your arms around it and keep up. It's not that a lot of people are just kind of sitting back and letting it happen. It is that those people working on this issue are a relatively lean team of exhausted experts."

The sobering chronology of the emerald ash borer makes Reaser's case. When Michigan extension agent David L. Roberts reported a lot of dead trees and his own dark suspicions, state and federal officials weren't much interested in helping him identify the problem. A year later, thanks to his persistence, the beetle was finally identified, and a local moratorium on shipping was declared, but it was hardly serious. A Maryland nursery took delivery of more than a hundred infested Michigan ash trees a few months later and sent them out to be planted. Two months after that, the feds finally issued an interim interstate quarantine on shipping ash trees. The genie was long out, however, and the borer had already spread through Michigan and Ohio.

Similarly, inspection regimes at U.S. ports are of the do-more-with-less school of self-delusion. Only 1 to 2 percent of the millions of cargo containers that enter U.S. ports each year are given a look. Compare that with a get-serious program: Dr. Carolyn Whyte, a biometrician and risk assessor with New Zealand's border management agency, says that in that country "each and every container is now unpacked in the presence of a person that has been trained and accredited."

Despite the shows of bipartisan support in the United States, the staggering high stakes and the rhetoric of growing urgency—"biopollution," "green cancer," and "global swarming" are making their way into currency—the pests have a commanding lead, and it's lengthening. We're still just shadowboxing.

Recent changes in U.S. trade rules, for example, require Hong Kong and Chinese shippers to certify that they have heat-treated or fumigated wood packing materials to ensure that more live beetles like the borers aren't coming over. But the follow-through has been listless. Late in 2003 the *Columbus (Ohio) Dispatch* quoted federal inspectors as saying, "Our officers don't place much faith in the fumigation certificates," and, "Some importers tell us that Chinese shippers will ask them if they want the fumigation certificate or the fumigation." A reporter and photographer for the newspaper said that officials in China refused their repeated requests to visit wood packaging fumigation sites.

Here are some more dots. You connect 'em:

- A larger relative of the Potomac snakehead fish has recently turned up in Wisconsin. In recent years snakeheads, a group native to Africa and Asia, have been found in a total of nine states from Maine to Hawaii.
- Federal agriculture officials have set up a national dragnet to try to contain a wheat virus from India called karnal bunt that has reached fields in Arizona, California, and Texas. If it gains a foothold, it will join Dalmatian toadflax, spotted knapweed, cheatgrass, and dozens of other colorfully named, imported scourges of U.S. agriculture. A Western Governors' Association report says that 70 million acres of the region's agricultural and natural lands have already been "lost" to non-native weed infestations and should be regarded as "national sacrifice areas."
- Veined rapa whelks from the Sea of Japan have taken up residence in the Chesapeake Bay. It's an aquatic neighborhood that already has a host of fast-spreading, introduced water weeds and an Asian disease that has all but demolished the native oyster population and the industry that depends upon it. The rapa whelk bores holes in native clams and oysters.
- In California and Oregon a newly introduced fungus whose pet name is "sudden oak death" has cut loose. It infects many other tree species, with as-yet unknown results. Foresters in the Appalachians are setting up monitoring efforts, but except for destroying affected trees and keeping fingers crossed, no one knows how to slow its spread.
- The Great Lakes states are trying to figure out how to keep the lakes free of the Asian silver carp, which can weigh up to fifty pounds and has the disconcerting habit of hurling itself at humans, nearly knocking some boaters overboard. The larger worry is that it will devastate native fisheries. Alien carp are introduced in many places in the United States to control alien weeds, and they have moved steadily northward, up the Mississippi. The Great

Lakes ecosystem has already been transformed by the Caspian Sea zebra mussel, which fouls boats and intake pipes and has to this date incurred costs in the hundreds of millions. Zebra mussels have been found in a Virginia quarry, too.

A common feature of the nasty biographies of many such pestilences is that they got here because of our preoccupation with promoting international trade, seemingly at all costs. More than twenty different federal agencies have a hand in the fight against invasives, and they are spending close to a billion dollars a year. Estimating conservatively, however, that's a mere 1 percent of the annual hit we are taking from this problem. Because the pests keep feeding and breeding, the costs are accelerating, quite naturally.

The National Invasive Species Council has already been criticized in two General Accountability Office (GAO) reports. Invasive species "are one of the most serious, yet least-appreciated, environmental threats of the 21st century," the GAO acknowledged, but added that the national commitment to fight it doesn't match the scale of the problem.

In any case, the bulk of the money we spend goes for mitigation of the invasives already here—certainly a necessity. But it's fantastically expensive and ineffective, compared with keeping them out, or setting up effective "early detection" to find them before they spread.

Another GAO criticism is that federal efforts lopsidedly target invasives affecting agriculture rather than forests, rangelands, lakes, rivers, and other natural areas, whose fate is just as crucial. No mystery there. Agricultural interests are far better organized and financed than environmental groups, and have much more clout, especially in the current administration.

A newly proposed federal "priority pest and disease" watch list, for example, is made up exclusively of invasives that affect agriculture. But the threat to natural areas is serious. Nearly half of all endangered and threatened species in the United

States are at risk because of invasives that are severely disrupting natural ecosystems.

What invasives are doing in the woods is "out of sight, out of mind" for most of us. Also, it's a contentious matter to try to assign dollar values to natural systems and their component parts. This means that ecosystem losses don't show up on the trade-balance sheets, even when they are vital to maintaining clean water and clean air—not to mention habitat for wild species. Even so, the tally of what we're losing in natural areas is getting hard to ignore.

In recent years, alien invasive insects and diseases have wiped out nearly all butternut trees and Fraser firs in the Appalachians—their eventual extinction in the wild has been predicted—and half or more of all native dogwoods. Native Eastern and Carolina hemlocks have been disappearing from Connecticut to the Carolinas during the past couple of decades because of a European insect, the hemlock woolly adelgid. It has turned up in Great Smoky Mountains National Park, and studies indicate that the prospects for survival of the groves of four-hundred-year-old hemlocks in the park are nil.

The Smokies national park draws more visitors than any other, outranking the Grand Canyon, Yellowstone, and Yosemite. At last count, more than a fifth of all of its plant species were aliens, including a couple of dozen that are invasive, aggressive, and impossible to get rid of. More are showing up all the time. The park's plant pest specialist, Kristine Johnson, once told me she has occasional bad dreams about kudzu.

At Shenandoah National Park, forest ecologist James Åkerson and his staff are battling Japanese knotweed, Asian bittersweet, ailanthus, Tree of Heaven, garlic mustard, multiflora rose, Chinese yam, mile-a-minute weed—more than two hundred alien plant species, many of which are spreading and, thus far, ineradicable.

A federal study of invasives has summed up the threat: "Concerns are increasing that the ecological changes overtaking the parks may be so severe that they will eliminate the very characteristics for which the parks were originally established. Unchecked, such changes eventually will eliminate the national parks' role as a caretaker of U.S. ecosystems and indigenous species."

To anthropomorphize just a little: the species we are up against are much clearer about their goals. For us, bugs and weeds are still way down on the worry list. Before it was detonated by the Gingrich Congress in the mid-1990s, the federal Office of Technology Assessment issued a report on its three-year study of the rising tide of invasives and what to do about them. A decade later, the study's project director, Phyllis Windle, said little had changed.

The strategy for the really valuable work of halting new invasions—as opposed to the sometimes hapless work of dealing with the established ones—seems to be to try to talk the problem to death. Windle, now with the Union of Concerned Scientists, has concluded that "When it really comes right down to which gets the higher priority, free trade or concerns about invasive species, we're still in the place we've always been. Free trade trumps everything else."

Indeed, despite all the militant words about invasives, federal policies are remarkably wobbly when trade might somehow be inhibited. Note the crippled ambivalence of this example from the "findings" that Congress passed along to guide implementation of the Plant Protection Act three years ago: "It is the responsibility of the Secretary [of Agriculture] to facilitate exports, imports, and interstate commerce in agricultural products and other commodities that pose a risk of harboring plant pests or noxious weeds in ways that will reduce, to the extent practicable, as determined by the Secretary, the risk of dissemination of plant pests or noxious weeds."

Several international trade agreements we have signed onto pay similar lip service to the need for protection against invasives, but trade predominates. World Trade Organization (WTO) pacts, for example, have usually been interpreted to require a species-by-species approach that throws the burden of proof onto any country that tries to limit the influx of invasives. In other words, critics say, you have to convict every species of its misdeeds individually—and let in all the ones whose cases are undecided, or unknown.

That's the "dirty list" approach, and the idea of methodically assembling a catalog of problematic species and then excluding them has an appealing, but illusory, logic. For one thing, there are ways to test species for safety, but the planet has millions. Who can test them all, against all their possible targets among natural systems and agricultural products, and then aggregate a list of bad actors?

For another, it is impossible to predict how an organism that finds itself in a new environment will behave. Many, relatively harmless on their native landscapes, can cause enormous damage on a new one, so testing is essential—and in practical terms, impossible.

The WTO and its member states, including the United States, have a legitimate concern here: that countries might camouflage unfair trade protection policies as "anti-invasives" policies. But as Windle and Faith Campbell of the American Lands Alliance have pointed out, the WTO's dismissive approach just about guarantees an ascending curve of new invasions in the future.

We're not the only victims. The United States is a major exporter of the same peril—destructive North American species that establish themselves in our marketplaces around the world. International trade agreements and our trade-above-all politics augur for more of this lethargy. They foster a species-at-a-time, innocent-until-proven-guilty approach.

If we mean to do a better job of keeping invasives out, then the "clean list" approach adopted during the 1990s by Australia and New Zealand, which has drastically cut the influx of biopollution, is a useful model. It, too, has a simple, compelling logic, and it actually works: allow only the organisms that are known to be safe to be imported, and arrange for the rest to be thoroughly tested for safety at the cost of the importer.

If they are proven to be unlikely to misbehave, they go on the "clean list." If something's not on that list, it stays out. New Zealand was recently deciding whether to deport noncitizens who try to smuggle in unexamined organisms.

In the book *A Plague of Rats and Rubbervines*, written for the UN-sponsored Global Invasive Species Program, author Yvonne Baskin has investigated how other countries are coping. She says that because the New Zealand–Australia "clean list" quarantine strategy is science-based, using elaborate risk assessments for all non-native species proposed for entry, the two countries have sidestepped trouble with the WTO. Aggrieved trading partners whose products have been banned would find it hard to make a credible claim that the process is either rigged or arbitrary.

New Zealand's is the tougher approach so far. Continuing problems with invasives in Australia—fire ants recently showed up in Queensland in nursery stock from the United States—are stoking the debate there over even more stringent controls, however.

In both countries, public education about the cost of invasives has been crucial. It has generated enough political will to oppose the laissez-faire notions of importers—the horticultural, seed, and pet trades and commercial growers, for example. The citizenry also has to have enough smarts to know that the expense and complications of a serious inspection system at the borders is a rare bargain, considering the scale of the risks.

There is a strong argument to be made that traders, rather than the rest of us, should pay for the inspection system as part of the cost of doing business safely. Because another common feature of most cases of invasives introductions is that the biopolluters don't pay to clean up the mess, when cleanups are even possible. The costs for lost crops or trashed forests and wetlands are borne instead by the public at large, or by those who suffer the damage directly.

So as a corollary, any country found inadvertently exporting, say, plant diseases on nursery stock, or wood-boring insects on wood pallets, should find that those products or shipping methods are banned until the problems are cleared up and paid for. Substituting other materials for wood pallets and packing materials, for instance, would eliminate the need for both fumigation and much of the inspection process.

The continuing importation of aquatic plants and animals in the ballast water dumped by ships in U.S. ports, from Seattle to the Chesapeake Bay, is just as serious a problem. As the Environmental Protection Agency (EPA) explains: "More than 21 billion gallons of ballast water are discharged in U.S. waters each year. This ballast water can contain living organisms taken up in a port half way around the world, which can invade the area where the water is discharged."

Indeed, that's where zebra mussels, rapa whelks, mitten crabs, and a growing list of other trouble species have come from. The EPA, meanwhile, petitioned by environmental groups to regulate ballast water discharges under the Clean Water Act, recently declined the job. It deferred instead to the Coast Guard, which has a voluntary, and ineffective, program.

The GAO reports on NISC also made some anguished comments about slow progress on the ballast water issue. No wonder. Over the last ten years, a new invader has been found in the Great Lakes, for example, about every seven to eight months, according to the Fish and Wildlife Service's regional office.

The biggest spender among federal agencies is APHIS, the Agricultural Plant Health Inspection Service, whose primary responsibilities include inspections of shipping and mounting an emergency response to new infestations. It's getting weary, at least in a financial sense. Pressured by the Office of Management and Budget, it wants to cut back aid to states and is asking the states to help foot the bill to fight invasives. Some states, though, blame all their new invasives problems on the lagging federal control efforts, and they are outraged.

A few years ago, a couple of entomologists analyzing the problem in a journal article broke free of the restrained language of science to write: "When the outrageous economic and ecological costs of the wanton spread of existing (invasives) and continued entry of new ones become common knowledge, it is inevitable that there will be a public outcry for action to mitigate the potentially dire consequences."

Out in the fields, the distress has long since been voiced. "Whatever we're doing now, it's not working," says Richard Kinney of the Florida Citrus Packers, who is a veteran of several federal advisory panels. "We've got a Band-aid over a cancer that is eating us up. Long-horned beetle? We ought to be enraged in this country over the potential devastation."

If that indignation finally emboldens the federal response, there's plenty to be done. We need more public education and volunteer anti-invasives campaigns, and both national and local programs for early detection of new invasions. We need an emphatic "rapid response" system to eradicate problem species before they become established. We need more stable, long-term funding for research on prevention and control. But the first order of business should be clear: Plug the holes in trade regulation that allow too much easy, free entry to too many new, unwelcome arrivals.

Swimming under
the Radar

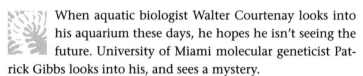When aquatic biologist Walter Courtenay looks into his aquarium these days, he hopes he isn't seeing the future. University of Miami molecular geneticist Patrick Gibbs looks into his, and sees a mystery.

They are both looking at specimens of the minnow-sized fish whose trademark name is Glofish—America's first genetically engineered pet. The merry-looking, human-created breed suddenly appeared in Florida pet stores in late 2003, a couple of weeks before a taken-by-surprise U.S. Food and Drug Administration declared that no formal review for environmental safety would be needed.

The FDA decision reversed an earlier policy that the agency would impose regulatory review on all introductions of genetically modified pets under the New Animal Drug Application (NADA) requirements of federal food, drug, and cosmetic legislation. Several national environmental groups filed suit against the U.S. Food and Drug Administration for failing to regulate the Glofish, and several scientists have also expressed concern about the regulatory process, as well as the fish. The California Fish and Game Commission has voted to ban sales of the Glofish in that state, as have Singapore and Japan.

The species *Danio rerio*, normally silver with black stripes and usually called zebra fish, is a native of the Ganges River region and a common choice for lab experiments. Modified with the genes of an Indo-Pacific sea anemone, the zebra fish becomes the patented, bright-red Glofish, which fluoresces under ultraviolet light. Yorktown Technologies of Austin, Texas, which owns the U.S. license to distribute the fish, says a green fluorescent version is slated to appear during the coming year.

There is only modest uncertainty whether escaped Glofish might multiply and derail native ecosystems, though U.S. waters are generally too cold for the fish to breed in. But Florida's Department of Agriculture, in the wake of the Glofish introduction, has appointed a task force to look into the potential environmental impacts of genetically modified fish generally.

Pam Fuller is a fisheries biologist at a federal research facility in Gainesville and the coauthor of a recent book on the five hundred–plus nonnative fish that have invaded U.S. waters. Without further study, she says, she is not fully convinced that the Glofish doesn't have some potential to establish reproducing populations in South Florida.

What are the risks? "Well, that's the problem," she says. "We don't know yet. Something like that should be studied a lot better than it has been, before we go playing around and selling things that could very well wind up in the wild. There are lots of other species that have been introduced in large numbers, and quite often they fail for years and years and then all of a sudden they are successful."

Walter Courtenay and some other researchers voice distress instead over the precedent set by what they see as the federal government's after-the-fact, laissez-faire treatment of a genetic novelty for sale to the public. By contrast, a modified "super salmon" that its promoters hope can be used as food has been under review by the FDA for several years. The FDA says that it will provide such oversight, for the time being, on a case-by-case basis.

The twenty-six-year-old entrepreneur Alan Blake, CEO of Yorktown Technologies, has said that he checked with the Environmental Protection Agency, the U.S. Fish and Wildlife Service, the Department of Agriculture, and the Food and Drug Administration and was told that they had no regulatory interest.

Neither Blake nor the FDA has any record of whom he might have phoned there when he was given a green light, according to an FDA spokesman. In any case, the spokesman adds, the agency was blindsided by a fast-moving technology and its own uncertainty—after more than a decade of mulling—over what to do about regulating transgenic animals.

The FDA learned of the planned introduction of the Glofish sometime in October, said John C. Matheson, senior regulatory review scientist at the FDA's Center for Veterinary Medicine. Yorktown Technologies then announced that the Glofish would go on sale in January 2003. The fish was actually available in Florida retail outlets in late November, and in other states soon after.

On the brink of those first sales, the Center for Food Safety, the Sierra Club, Consumers' Union, Greenpeace, and other environmental groups demanded that the FDA intervene to forestall the Glofish's retail debut, pending a safety review. They pointed out that Singapore and Japan had already halted sales of fluorescing zebra fish, and that many similar new bioengineered products are on the horizon. "The floodgates are yours to close," their letter stated. California's fish and game commission then voted to ban Glofish sales in the state, citing ethical concerns about genetic engineering for trivial uses.

A couple of weeks after the fish was already on sale elsewhere, the FDA issued a one-paragraph statement that concluded: "In the absence of a clear risk to the public health, the FDA finds no reason to regulate these particular fish." Matheson explained that the phrase "public health" should be interpreted broadly, to include environmental health.

"I think folks are continuing to consider what's the best way," Matheson said the day after the statement was released. "We would have liked to have heard from [Alan Blake] sooner, but I'm not sure there are any legal obligations on him." The FDA review, Matheson said, consisted of dialogues with staff members of several federal agencies who might be concerned with the introduction of a new variety of fish. No written records were kept, no reports were issued, and the names of the conferees are being withheld from the public.

Some scientists and other government regulators were also caught up in the uncertainties. Blake asked at least five prominent researchers to write letters vouching for the environmental safety of the Glofish. All the letters became part of the regulatory process in California and were among those posted on the Glofish Web site by way of reassurance for the public that the product is environmentally safe.

Two of the writers have financial ties to the Glofish project. Two others say that despite their confidence in its safety, the new fish should have triggered a federal regulatory review before going on sale—and they were taken by surprise when it didn't. Their experience illustrates some paradoxes for scientists when they are asked for advice in the absence of regulatory oversight.

Bill Muir, a professor of genetics at Purdue, and fishery science professor Eric Hallerman, who specializes in population genetics and risk assessment at Virginia Tech, volunteered to review, gratis, data that Blake provided on the Glofish's safety, and they have no financial ties to the product.

Based on data that Alan Blake provided, Muir's letter concludes that "one would expect natural selection to eliminate the transgene regardless of where it escaped or was released." Hallerman characterized the possibility of ecological impacts from escaped Glofish as "remote."

But both scientists are concerned that such letters could be used to substitute for careful scientific review. "The Glofish really didn't go through any federal review process as far as I understand it," Muir said. "Everything that has an environmental impact should have some sort of regulatory overview. Even children's toys and children's clothes have that—anything that has a potential of moderate risk."

Muir said that at the time he wrote the letter, he thought the

U.S. Food and Drug Administration intended to regulate transgenic pets. "To be quite frank, I thought they were going to be
shut down by the FDA before they got released," he said.

"I just assumed that somewhere along the line Fish and
Wildlife or APHIS [the Department of Agriculture's Animal
and Plant Health Inspection Service] or FDA, one of those
three, would tag onto it, claim jurisdiction and do a ruling
on it. And I thought the ruling would be a stay, to say, 'Well,
wait a minute now, it's probably going to be okay, but we want
more data.'"

Hallerman served with Muir on a National Research Council
panel whose 2002 report pointed out scientific concerns posed
by animal biotechnology and gaps in federal oversight of bioengineering. That report included the supposition—based on
past practice—that the FDA would initiate a premarket review
of any project like the Glofish, and the report added that several other federal statutes could also be invoked as the basis for
a review of a transgenic fish.

"I think there is a real issue here," Hallerman said. "This Glofish fell right through the cracks of federal oversight." Without
federal review, he added, biotechnology "becomes a state issue, and then there's fifty different regulatory regimes."

Hallerman said that he had wanted to be a responsible friend
of the regulatory process in California. While writing his letter
on the Glofish, he had several concerns, though. One was "the
notion whether people would think I was in Alan's pocket,
doing it because I was wired into the profits. In fact, someone
flamed me in an email about that and made me very angry."

A series of testimonial letters is unsatisfactory as the basis
for review, Hallerman said. The first hurdle for the Glofish
should have been an environmental assessment, to determine
whether a full-blown environmental impact statement review
needed to be performed. "It's not without misgivings that I
allowed Alan to use the letter, and it's not without misgivings
that I have allowed it to remain up [on the Web site]. Depend-

ing how this shakes out, I might ask him to bring it down," he said.

"There should at least have been an application process, a hearing in Washington and an advisory board weighing in. That can all be done expeditiously in a slam-dunk case like this."

The feds also failed even to glance at another potential source of trouble, according to the University of Miami's Patrick Gibbs. He has tested the DNA of Glofish and is concerned about genetic material he found that he says was not reviewed for safety, including genes that code for antibiotic resistance. Gibbs is no enviro-freak. He is a proponent of commercial development of transgenics—also called genetically modified organisms—and has been trying to bring his own to market for several years.

"I want the regulatory people to look into this thing responsibly and make a decision based upon the facts," he wrote in an email to colleagues. "As far as I can tell NOBODY knows what is in the Glofish. And yet the FDA (sort of) OK'd it. . . . And it's a major precedent-setter. Essentially, the FDA is saying we regulate it if you eat it or inject it, but not necessarily if you touch it or the environment comes in contact with it."

One of the recipients of the email was another geneticist, Perry Hackett, of Discovery Genomics, Inc., who is currently on leave from the University of Minnesota. Hackett has been involved in the development of the Glofish. He introduced its creator, Zhiyuan Gong at the University of Singapore, to the U.S. contacts who have licensed him to sell the fish here.

Hackett's email accuses Gibbs of "playing on the scientific ignorance of the general population to spoil what should be an interesting example of the power of modern molecular genetics that everyone can understand. . . . I doubt all this effort that you are putting into this issue will lead to much."

Walter Courtenay, the USGS research fishery biologist and invasive species specialist, looks at the three vivid little Glofish that he bought in a Gainesville pet store with strong misgivings. "I don't want to see any more of these. I hope this is the end of it," he says. "Right now, there is no regulatory process at all."

During most of his career as an aquatic biologist, Courtenay has studied the lifeways of alien fish species let loose in North American waters, including the ways they disrupt ecosystems and devastate native fish populations. He was summoned in 2002 to advise when voracious Asian snakehead fishes made it out of someone's home collection to multiply in a Maryland pond.

They threatened to join introduced carp, swamp eels, nutria, zebra mussels, rapa whelks, and hundreds of other destructive, introduced organisms that thrive in the United States, especially in Florida.

"The problem with the Glofish is not this one," he said. "It's what's next. What scares me the most is that if they start modifying fish that turn out to be predators and released into the environment—which people will do; they always release their pets, for some reason or other—it could cause serious problems."

Clones in the Cathedral

At an industrial park in Walnut Creek, California, technicians and robots are sorting through the 550 million base pairs of genetic code in poplar DNA to sequence a tree genome for the first time. They are poised to unlock a fine, full toolbox for the work of genetic engineering in trees.

In Vermont, a group called Action for Social and Ecological Justice has just kicked off a national campaign to force companies to ban research on genetically engineered (GE) trees. The Sierra Club, the World Wildlife Fund, and the American Lands Alliance, among others, have called for a moratorium on the commercialization of GE trees.

In Washington, a federal agency with key responsibility for judging the biological safety of GE trees is preparing its response for Congress to a report by the National Research Council (NRC), which cites a long list of misgivings about the agency's work.

Though results from most projects are either uncertain or years off, the research is well advanced on GE trees for industry and agriculture, and on some that might be good for the environment. Engineered trees may grow faster, or more compactly, or they may be more cheaply converted into pulp and paper. They may incorporate genes that confer insect resistance on an apple tree, or drought resistance on a pine.

"There is a major thrust on growing proteins in plants, and trees may be a vehicle for that," says biotech industry consultant David Duncan, formerly with GE research giant Monsanto. Growing interferon for hepatitis C therapy, for example, or growing insulin, or human serum albumin, important as a blood thickener in post-operative uses. It is currently derived from human blood and is very expensive.

More than two hundred notices of field trials have been filed with federal regulators for lab-engineered fruit, nut, and forest trees—also known as genetically modified, biotech, or transgenic trees. But aside from a virus-resistant, bushlike papaya tree grown in Hawaii, no one has yet sought regulatory approval for commercial use of a gene-altered tree.

"Maybe soon," says Vincent Chiang, codirector of the forest biotechnology group at North Carolina State University. Like others in this field of research, he feels little certainty about how the regulatory climate for GE trees will evolve. "But if we don't consider that factor, if we could grow transgenic trees just like we grow ordinary trees now, in two years those trees could be put into the ground, so we could have wood available to a pulp mill in six years," Chiang says.

One of his projects has been to engineer trees to produce less lignin, which is expensive to remove during the process of turning pulp into wood. The process could save industry tens of millions of dollars per year. It has been licensed to Arborgen, a $60-million joint research venture of the International Paper Company, the MeadWestvaco Corporation, and two New Zealand firms. Arborgen estimates that, if tests go very well, the product could be ready for the market in a decade.

Tinkering with tree DNA presents some gnarled issues for research and for public policy, however:

- The potential for gene flow from GE trees to wild forests.
- The possibility of inadvertently creating "Frankentrees," in the activist's vernacular, that would outcompete native varieties and disrupt native ecosystems.
- Managing GE trees that incorporate pesticides so resistant strains of insects, diseases, and plants won't quickly develop.

- Gauging the effect of pesticidal and other GE trees on "nontarget" species—other insects, plants, and animals.

Casting an uncertain light over all GE tree projects is the fact that human society tends to revere trees, and to both embrace and mistrust new technologies. Research labs and plantations associated with GE trees have been vandalized and firebombed in Oregon, Washington, and England. These tactics, rejected by nearly all environmental groups, are nonetheless taken by some scientists as a rough indicator of public malaise about the prospect of transgenic trees.

"When you start doing genetic manipulation of what is widely considered to be a wild species, it raises a whole different set of issues than if you are doing it with agricultural plants," says molecular ecologist Stephen DiFazio of the Oak Ridge National Laboratory. "So even if there isn't a strong, credible scientific risk, there is a public perception issue that can be quite substantial." DiFazio has studied patterns of gene flow from plantation poplars to wild relatives in Oregon.

"You hear people refer to forests as nature's cathedrals. Scientists I know who are working with trees have those feelings, too," says Gerald Tuskan, a senior scientist at Oak Ridge. Tuskan is part of a group of international collaborators that is midway through the draft sequencing of the poplar genome. The project's chief sponsor is the U.S. Department of Energy.

"We're blurring the distinction between what's natural and what's man-made," says Alan McQuillan, a forestry management professor at the University of Montana. "Where do we draw the line? From an extreme position there's nothing left that's natural. From a more moderate position, there are still things in the world that are pretty much natural, pretty much unaffected by humans. If I had a choice, I would oppose it."

For some advocates of the technology, the fact that GE plants are regulated more closely than other plants is especially vexing. They want regulators and the public to distinguish the process of creating GE trees—which they say is value-neutral—

from the products. A tree that may or may not be good for the environment should be regulated accordingly, they argue, not on the basis of propaganda that stigmatizes its origins in a lab. They cite a scientific consensus: As the National Academy of Sciences has stated, introducing GE organisms "poses no risks different from the introduction of unmodified organisms and organisms modified by other mechanisms."

Some worry that an onerous "regulatory load" that mixes politics with science has chilled investment interest, and, under the guise of oversight, threatens to suffocate the infant industry along with the research it supports.

But opponents claim that the GE tree technology itself is unacceptable: It's too powerful to be relinquished to multinational corporation patent licensees whose environmental commitments are just lip service. Or it's too complex for our publicly funded science—haphazard, misdirected, and malnourished as it is—to be able to predict the potential for catastrophic side effects. Or it's too much of a threat for cheerleading federal agencies to be allowed to regulate it.

There is also a middle-ground discussion. Its boundaries are defined on one side by a call for an indefinite moratorium on commercial development of GE trees. This would last until important scientific issues are resolved and a credible and authoritative federal regulatory apparatus is in place. Faith Campbell of the American Lands Alliance says of the government's current role that "there's a lot of words there, but most of the time it seems to boil down to next to nothing."

Then there's the question of whether GE plants should be burdened more than conventionally bred crops by regulatory oversight. Campbell notes that the NRC justifies the scrutiny—and recommends far more—for GE and non-GE plants both, to ensure biological safety.

The other side of this range of thought favors commercial development of demonstrably benign GE tree innovations, as a public confidence-builder. It also calls for extensive monitoring, under an improved regulatory system. DiFazio, for one, suggests controlled commercial releases with traits that carry negligible risk. Then long-term, large-scale studies can chart how far the genes disperse in the wild, and provide answers about invasiveness.

One difference between GE trees—still in regulatory limbo—and the many other transgenic plants that are already approved for commercial use is that, unlike corn and soybeans, trees endure. Also, they exert a dominant influence in many ecosystems on the basis of size alone.

Just as important is their evolutionary history. Most crops have been domesticated for thousands of years and are now markedly different from their wild relatives. But the genetic makeup of forest trees, even those grown as row crops on industrial plantations, has scarcely been altered by humans.

"We're starting with organisms that are, today, exactly as they were sixty thousand years ago, or millions of years ago in some cases," Tuskan says. "There hasn't been a lot of selective pressure placed on them, for many good reasons. They are long-lived, they are difficult to work with, their reproductive structures sometimes occur hundreds of feet off the ground."

Which means that genetically engineered pine or poplar trees, for example, may hybridize with wild relatives more easily. "With trees, the wild species can be just down the road, or just around a riverbend," Tuskan says. Clouds of wind-borne tree pollen can disperse over long distances and enormous areas.

Such concerns put a premium on finding a way to engineer sterility into trees, though few if any experts have concluded that this could be made 100 percent reliable. "The holy grail of biotech improvement is a tree that is an elite producer, with a gene construct that prevents the tree from pollinating," says biotech consultant Duncan. "First and foremost is the whole issue of controlling the potential for outcrossing.

"If industry wants to engineer herbicide tolerance or insect protection or fiber modification into a tree species, then they'd be well served either from a regulatory standpoint or just from a public acceptance standpoint to address that issue. It is a key enabling technology."

Duncan calls Oregon State geneticist Steve Strauss the world's foremost authority on modifying trees so they won't reproduce. Strauss says that at least some gene flow from biotech tree plantations to wild forests is likely to be inevitable, but of little consequence: no deleterious effects, and no accidental creation of a super-tree.

He rejects the possibility that engineered trees might behave like invasive exotics, because they are "orders of magnitude more complex a unit to introduce into a new environment than a single gene." For example, the exotic melaleuca tree, a severely disrupting invasive in Florida, presents a whole suite of adaptations evolved over tens of millions of years. "Those are not single-gene traits," Strauss notes.

This view is shared by the Biotechnology Regulatory Service, the section of the federal Animal and Plant Health Inspection Service (APHIS), whose job is to judge the biological safety of GE plants, including trees. "We don't necessarily believe that introduction of an alien species onto a new continent is a good or useful model from which to approach genetically engineered plants," says John Turner, acting supervisor for biotechnology risk assessment. "In that case, you have an entirely new organism being introduced. How it will behave is very unpredictable. In this case, we are dealing with plants that have been here for a long time, and it is usually changing a single trait. We think that's very different."

Perhaps not, however. The NRC panel that reviewed APHIS's work on regulating GE plants rejected the assumption that single-gene changes have small ecological effects. Its recent report also rejected any strict distinction between alien invasives and transgenic plants on the basis of the environmental hazards they may present. "Introduction of biological novelty can have unintended and unpredicted effects" on ecosystems, the NRC report cautioned.

In poplar, for example—the tree of choice for a wide range of

GE projects—"the addition of a single transgene that improves some ecological characteristic could increase the weediness or invasiveness of the species, and these risks merit evaluation."

Other scientists echo the NRC's concerns about ecosystem effects, even from trees bearing only single-gene modifications. University of Wisconsin insect ecologist Kenneth Raffa, for example, has written, "The general lesson is that when you transfer a technology from closed, controlled conditions to open complex systems, there are almost always unforeseen parameters that affect system behavior."

Raffa and colleagues have also written that unanticipated indirect effects are a "realistic" risk of introducing transgenic trees and could reduce populations of predators, parasites, scavengers, pollinators, and endangered or valued species.

Raffa believes that the technology holds promise, but he finds the argument that genetically accelerated domestication of trees will make them feeble competitors in the wild unconvincing. "There are so many examples of organisms that are not competitive in one environment being extremely competitive in a different environment. . . . We have to build attributes into the plants themselves and into the growing systems, to provide safeguards," he says.

Raffa knows of no basis for the assurance that native gene pools will swamp accidentally introduced genetic novelties, either: "Accidental introductions of organisms have completely altered ecosystems, and often the particular organism introduced is almost unheard-of, under very low densities on its native landscape. We don't have that kind of predictive power."

Trees may be engineered to produce *Bacillus thuringiensis* (BT), a soil microbe that in turn produces a toxin that kills or repels insects. Another recurring concern is the likelihood of a steady increase in insect resistance to BT toxin. This could make a highly valuable natural insecticide completely useless and perhaps invite an explosion of some insect populations currently held in check.

"If you have BT in a tree or corn, you will be able to kill insects," says Bernd Blossey, a Cornell University plant ecologist. "There's just no question that you might have a short-term reduction in pesticide use, but you might have a long-term disaster. I don't know that, but I am obviously concerned about it, because we already know that there is resistance developing against BT." In a process similar to the one now occurring with antibiotics and human health, "careless use would mean throwing away one of the most potent insecticides we have," Blossey adds.

One means of delaying the development of resistance would be to plant swaths of normal, unaltered trees alongside GE plantations. These would serve as refuges for nonresistant insects, and the admixture of the two groups would stave off resistance, at least for a time.

Compliance and enforcement are a sticking point. Experience with farmers who were supposed to plant refuges for BT row crops has not been reassuring, Blossey says. "They have a very short-term benefit if they plant their entire field with transgenics, instead of giving a quarter of their field for the insects to devour. People are smart. They count their pennies. They have to."

Scientists who are relatively untroubled by the possibility of "contamination" of wild gene pools with an influx of human-altered genes may advocate long-term monitoring of GE trees and surrounding ecosystems just the same. "That's the way to do it, to tell you the truth," DiFazio says, "because these ecological questions are so complex. You can do preliminary small-scale tests of invasiveness but the level of inference that you can have from those tests is extremely limited." Tree plantations that are only harvested every fifty years should be monitored during that whole period, he said.

But discussions about long-term monitoring and other safety measures that depend on voluntary compliance have to take into account a record of breaches that have already occurred during the short history of transgenic plants. Along with the ill-famed StarLink episode (in which foods containing unapproved, genetically modified corn were sold commercially), some pharmaceutical-producing biotech corn was accidentally allowed to grow in Nebraskan soybean fields recently. The same company responsible for potentially contaminating the soybeans, Prodigene, was required to burn 155 acres of Iowa corn that might have cross-pollinated with a GE strain. Still other biotech firms were fined for violating Environmental Protection Agency regulations for field tests of insect-resistant GE corn in Hawaii.

If the biological safety of transgenic trees relies on promises of elaborate planning and long-term vigilance, however, who will ensure that rules are followed? Critics juxtapose the relatively short attention span of humans—the ebb and flow of business conditions, agency budgets, and antiregulatory politics—against the abiding nature of trees.

The EPA and the Food and Drug Administration help regulate GE plants that generate food, feed, pesticides, and pharmaceuticals, but the focus of the National Research Council's recent report is APHIS, a branch of the Department of Agriculture that regulates any genetically engineered plant.

North Carolina State University entomologist Fred Gould, who chaired the NRC panel that produced the report, characterized its recommendations for APHIS as "a means to help improve a functioning system." And the current regulatory process has its supporters, such as Arborgen, the private enterprise GE tree research consortium.

APHIS examines GE plants closely, says Les Pearson, Arborgen's director of regulatory affairs. "For us, that's just part of the landscape. There's a lot of learning for the public to do to understand about transgenic trees, and so that's perhaps appropriate."

Adds Maud Hinchee, Arborgen's chief technical officer: "Private enterprise works with regulatory agencies, and we have a lot of faith in them. I think we have some of the best regulatory processes in the world, and other countries mimic the methods used in the U.S."

But the NRC report took sharp exception to much of the way APHIS evaluates the safety of transgenics. It stressed that rigorous scientific risk analysis is not just the basis for good policy. It also "serves as evidence to the public that the decision-making agencies are deserving of their trust," Gould wrote.

The NRC committee reached these conclusions:

- APHIS usually relies on the least rigorous of five different levels of evidence used to produce its risk assessments of transgenics.
- Meeting higher standards would enhance the agency's regulatory legitimacy.
- The APHIS section responsible for regulating transgenics is underfunded and understaffed, and its personnel are overworked. Their collective scientific training does not match their regulatory responsibilities.
- The agency has no authority to monitor transgenics after they have been approved for commercial use.
- The agency's deregulation of them is absolute, with no further authority to monitor the GE plants. But detailed long-term monitoring of ecosystem impacts, over a number of years and locations, is needed.
- Individual GE traits that are approved for commercial use because they are presumed safe can be combined later in a single type of plant—this is called "gene stacking"—without further scrutiny by APHIS, though the traits could interact in novel ways.
- There should be "substantial increases in public-sector investment" for research on the opportunities and risks associated with transgenics.
- APHIS should begin to include any potential impacts of transgenic plants on farming practices or systems in its judgments of whether a transgenic should be deregulated.

All of which, the NRC report emphasizes, would require some major changes at APHIS. The larger political context, of course, is an era of budget cuts and diminished interest in government regulation of business. "Society so far—or maybe it's just the people who dole out the cash—have been unwilling to fund what is really necessary in terms of some of the long-term studies," says Blossey, who served on the NRC committee.

"One of the things we struggled with in the study is that we don't have good data on how organismal diversity in North America is being affected by anything: drought, herbicides or other pesticide use, or habitat loss. "When we don't know that, it is very, very difficult to do something smart. . . . I don't think there is any data that would allow us to do a rigorous assessment of what transgenic tree plantations would actually do at the level required for commercial approval," he added.

"What we have to be really careful about is that both sides could be right or could be wrong. As a scientist I always like to look at what the data are telling me, and I get very, very little data to look at. Neither side is arguing about data, but about their gut feelings, which makes coming down with a good scientific assessment extremely difficult."

For the University of Wisconsin's Ken Raffa, one essential feature of a good regulatory system for GE trees would be a testing process that incorporates ecosystem concerns. That would entail a lot of change in how research money is allocated. As anyone who competes for grant money can testify, Raffa has written, the successful applicants propose tight, narrowly focused experiments that can be conducted under controlled conditions with quick results, using organisms that lend themselves to simple kinds of measurement. "Unfortunately, the key questions about environmental safety are long-term and complex, and they operate across several species and multiple levels of the food web," he adds.

The NRC report also faulted APHIS's regulatory activity for its opacity. So much data is kept secret as "confidential business information" (CBI) that even the NRC committee itself was stymied at times in evaluating the agency's rulings. "Under this CBI stamp, all manner of data are hidden from public

view and even from independent scientific scrutiny," the report said. APHIS's regulatory process for transgenics "should
be made significantly more transparent and rigorous by en-
hanced scientific peer review, solicitation of public input, and
. . . more explicit presentation of data, methods, analyses and
interpretations."

Environmentalists have proposed that the needed research
should be bankrolled by the technology's sponsors, but it
should be insulated from their possible influence, and from
APHIS itself, which they see as strongly influenced by agribusi-
ness. Several researchers concerned about regulatory credibility support some version of such measures.

For Les Pearson of Arborgen, however, the current system is
fair and maintains the needed protection for proprietary information. The regulators have the data they need, he said, and
"the general public has a lot of faith in them, and understands
that there is some information that needs to be confidential."
Pearson said he is comfortable with the amount of transparency now: "There are certainly things that we need to keep
proprietary. So at this point, I wouldn't want to change that."

David Duncan, the industry consultant, says, "Private industry does not want an environmental catastrophe. They
don't want a non-efficacious product in the marketplace, for
obvious reasons. They have a huge liability. They have their
very company at risk if something should go awry."

But Blossey contends that secrecy militates against credibility, and he doubts claims for safety by the companies doing
the research. "We need to have the data from out in the field
where they have their experimental plantings," he says, "and
it has to be published and made accessible for critique by independent scientists." He is hopeful that more transparency
could lead to a common understanding about what should be
monitored.

As for the claim that corporate liability can be relied on to
guarantee the biosafety of GE trees, "I don't think the corpora-

tions have done a wonderful job in giving long-term steward-ship. Particularly not the forest industry," Blossey says.

Steve Strauss directs the Tree Genetic Engineering Research Cooperative at Oregon State, some of whose work has been funded by the forest products industry. He says that corporate interest in keeping proprietary knowledge private will have to be reconciled with the intense level of public interest in GE trees, if progress toward commercialization is to be made.

"Companies give lip service to doing things more openly and transparently," he said. "I don't see much of it happening yet. I don't know if it will happen. They have a whole different culture, a different mind-set.

"What really bugs activists is, they don't trust corporations, and they're convinced that this technology wouldn't be done if it weren't for corporations seeking profits. They just ignore the fact that there's a lot of good uses for biotechnology, ap-propriately chosen and carefully developed. The activists like to beat themselves into a frenzy by thinking it's all multina-tional mind control, and it looks that way. There's grounds for those concerns. The companies don't share what they do very well, and that generates paranoia. But the next step the activ-ists take is to demonize the whole technology."

And, "The nay-sayers want everybody to believe that there ought to be thirty years of testing before a product can go on the market," Duncan says. Well, you've just killed the industry if you require that."

Some of the nay-sayers are demanding a good bit more. "The one way they could with certainty prove that this would be an innocuous technology if it were to contaminate native forests," says Brad Hash of Action for Social and Ecological Justice (ASEJ), "is to grow genetically engineered trees that ex-press every trait that's being researched. Continue that growth through the entire life of the tree, have it die and decompose into the soil, then conduct soil- and water-quality sampling to determine whether this is truly benevolent." ASEJ is part of a campaign to demand an indefinite moratorium on GE tree research at the International Paper Company. The hoped-for repercussions would halt such research at all U.S. companies, Hash says.

Anti-biotech activists face some paradoxes if they reject GE trees forever, though. Some of these innovations might prove to be good for the environment. Experiments are under way to engineer trees whose roots will take toxins up from polluted soil. Fast-growing populations of GE trees might ease the global pressure to log wild forests. Trees might be engineered so as to sequester more carbon and mitigate global warming. Insect-resistant trees could reduce the need to spray pesticides or to use harsh chemicals during the wood-pulping process.

Some of these claims are dismissed by GE opponents as wag-the-dog public relations maneuvers—"greenwashing" designed to divert attention toward pleasant-sounding minor details and away from major hazards. They find other such possibilities to be too speculative, and far too dependent on long-term, shifting economic and technological factors, and much less tangible than the hazards. But the prospect of restoring chestnut, dogwood, hemlock, butternut, or elm trees to American forest ecosystems via genetic engineering seems less easy to shrug off.

One such project is making halting progress in labs at the State University of New York (SUNY) Environmental Science and Forestry School in Syracuse and at the University of Georgia. Work is under way there to create a transgenic chestnut, resistant to the blight that erased the tree from the Appalachian ecoregion during the last century.

SUNY molecular biologist William Powell and Charles Maynard of the forestry department have spent the last twelve years trying to incorporate two or three genes that would confer resistance into chestnut. One encodes a gene from wheat, used to detoxify a destructive acid that blight fungus produces. "We've done all the pieces but we haven't got everything together to get the gene in and regenerate the whole plant, Powell says. "I think within this decade, we will have a resistant tree."

The New York group is collaborating with Scott Merkle, a tree biotechnologist at the University of Georgia, Athens, whose specialties are propagating trees from cellular material and developing gene transfer techniques—both very difficult with chestnuts.

On these campuses, funding from government agencies has plummeted since 9/11. Three-fourths of the annual budget that keeps Powell's work going now—about $75,000—has been donated by Arborgen as a public service project, along with a like amount for Merkle's research.

Biotech tree researchers are excited about the sequencing of the poplar genome, but the excitement is tempered by frustration: Will they be able to put these powerful new tools to use?

The project will lead over time to a matching of genes with their functions. In turn, tree health and growth play a crucial role in many ecosystems, "so we will begin applying that knowledge to ecosystems, to understand how they function and what's required," says the Oak Ridge National Laboratory's Gerald Tuskan. On the industrial side, "We should be able to take what is essentially an undomesticated organism—poplar, loblolly pine, or Douglas fir—and accelerate its domestication so that it is better suited to the environments in which a company may be trying to produce," he says.

But as the research clarifies, public and regulatory acceptance of its applications remains a foggy uncertainty. "I know that there are commercial crop trees, economically viable right now—that have not been released because of those pressures," Tuskan says. "I don't think it comes down to pointing fingers at APHIS. They certainly are the bottleneck, or the gatekeepers, but I think there would be public outcries if that wasn't in place.

"Now I'd hate to see this become a permanent situation. It has caused delays in the transfer of technology into commercial applications. I hope that it's only a temporary glitch where we stop, take a look around, take an inventory of where we are, and then make a rational decision. If this becomes the permanent policy, then I think it's heavily flawed."

Strauss offers a back-handed salute to the success of activists who oppose GE trees. "In terms of round one of the war, they won and we lost. . . . I don't see how you can think of it any other way. There's much more and much better to come, but it's going to face more difficulty because of where we are."

University of Montana forestry professor Alan McQuillan shares the sense of resignation, but from the opposite perspective: The commercial development of GE trees, he says, has overridden any chance for a thorough debate. The commercial development of GE trees is taken as assumed. "I think that society has made the decision that it's doing it," he says. "It's not just the United States, it's global."

Brad Hash, on the eve of the new campaign to halt GE tree research, gives better odds for an extended debate. Bids for commercial development may be several years off, he noted. That offers time to mobilize public opinion "so that we don't get into the situation that GE food is in. So that we don't have to stuff the genie back in the bottle. Once the organism has produced and spread the seed, you're not going to be able to recall it."

In late 2005, the Department of Agriculture's Office of Inspector General delivered a stinging rebuke to APHIS, its own agency, for its failure to regulate field trials of GM crops, and risking biological pollution of the environment.

The report charged that APHIS personnel didn't know the locations of field trials they had approved, rules violations went unnoticed, experimental plantings went uninspected as required, and assurances that experimental GM crops were destroyed as required were lacking. APHIS responded, as it had nearly three years earlier, that reforms were under way.

Conservation Genetics I

There wasn't much doubt that the corpses in the bag federal investigators dropped on George Amato's desk were primates. Beheaded, quartered, and smoked, their still-attached hands and feet indicated as much.

The question for geneticist Amato was, what kind of primates? The feds had seized the contraband bushmeat at JFK from a flight that came in from West Africa. It had been smuggled here to provide complicit or ill-informed African émigrés a traditional meal from home.

"They asked if we could help them to identify the species," he recalls, "so we took tissue samples, and sequenced the DNA." The results were compared with DNA sequences published on the Internet. They turned out to be a red colobus monkey and a couple of mangabeys—a diverse group of Central African primates—all of which are protected as either threatened or endangered under international treaties. The case is still under investigation.

This kind of genetics detective work is increasingly common, and not only at Amato's Wildlife Conservation Society lab, where bear gall bladders, rhino horns, and various skins and antlers have been assayed. The U.S. Fish and Wildlife Service runs its own forensics crime lab in Ashland, Oregon, with eight genetics specialists on staff. Harvard's Stephen Palumbi and colleagues set up portable labs in Tokyo hotel rooms each year, where they sequence the DNA of whale meat sampled at

Tokyo restaurants and markets. Some of it, they've shown, is from illegally harvested, endangered whales.

Forensics is just one of an array of developing uses for molecular genetics in conservation. They range from distinguishing previously unrecognized species to using gene markers to trace the behavior, demographic patterns, evolutionary history, and genealogies of organisms. And as many wildlife populations decline and become isolated, managed breeding to maintain genetic diversity becomes more urgent, and more carefully choreographed.

Dad's Fingerprints

Genetic research has begun to tease loose at least a few of the knots in rare species management projects. One has puzzled ecologists who are trying to revive and extend the tiny remnants of American tall-grass prairies. There, the rapidly vanishing Mead's milkweed has become a kind of prairie ecosystem poster child.

Some of the protected populations occur on old hayfields that had been mowed each spring. Milkweed growth was vigorous, but flowering and seed-setting was unaccountably weak—an alarming trait because the plant is already so rare.

Another complication arose from the fact that milkweed can spread vegetatively, sending up cloned stems at varying distances from the parent plant. Short of ripping up and sorting through a densely woven subterranean mat of root systems, there seemed to be no way, until recently, to determine which stems belonged to which parent plants or for that matter, how many plants there were in a given area.

But one researcher has been able to solve the puzzle above ground. Using a collaborator's new, rapid, high-resolution DNA analysis of leaf samples, conservation biologist Marlin Bowles of the Morton Arboretum in Chicago assembles genetic maps of milkweed fields.

They've revealed that mowing has, over a long period, selected against the normal multitude of smaller plants. Instead, mowing leads to fewer, but more extensive, milkweed clones. Milkweed can't self-pollinate, so these fields of a few single, large plants weren't generating many flowers and seeds.

Bowles also found that fields that are burned instead of mowed have a far higher number of distinct milkweed plants per acre. That in turn promotes more flowers and sexual reproduction, thus more genetic diversity and adaptability within the population. Burning is now the strategy of choice for managing the species. Milkweed populations are setting seed again, and sexual reproduction has resumed, yielding better survival odds.

A longer-term mystery has also lurked in the behavior of the well-known chimpanzee population in Gombe Stream National Park, Tanzania. It has been studied for nearly forty years, beginning with the work of Jane Goodall, and one result, says geneticist Mary Ashley of the University of Illinois, is that "these animals have no privacy at all."

Just the same, she told a recent symposium on conservation genetics, it has been impossible until recently to determine who among the males is actually fathering most of the babies. A related question—the effectiveness of the chimps' strategies for avoiding inbreeding—has also remained unanswered.

These closest of man's animal relatives are highly promiscuous, and females may copulate a hundred times during the estrus cycle, sometimes with every adult male of the community. Now, DNA "fingerprints" in fecal and hair samples have sorted out paternity, and gauged the level of inbreeding, without disturbing the animals.

"One of the most important contributions that can be made by molecular genetics or biotechnology in conservation is simply to supply a new tool to ecologists and population biologists who are doing work on species that we're trying to protect," she told the symposium.

"Measuring dispersal, survival, recruitment, or life history, we can get some new and sometimes important information useful for management."

Eight Texas Females

The new techniques are also informing age-old debates among systematists—biologists whose work is to differentiate species. Both "lumpers" and "splitters" can marshal powerful genetic evidence for establishing the existence of new species, subspecies, and populations, or for collapsing what are believed to be distinct species into fewer groups.

Such discussions may have major consequences for endangered wildlife management programs because they are, after all, geared to the rarity of particular species. Late in 2000, for example, molecular geneticists, relying in part on DNA sampling of century-old museum specimens, demonstrated that a population of fewer than a thousand Northern right whales in the North Pacific is genetically distinct from Atlantic populations. Their findings argue that this unique species, newly discerned, should be protected as endangered under U.S. law and international treaties.

The genetics of the Florida panther, on the other hand, have helped justify interbreeding them with another panther population as part of a last-ditch survival plan. Government rare species management policy, especially at the federal level, is heavily weighted against tinkering with native natural systems by hybridizing different subspecies—even to fend off local extinctions.

Only about thirty Florida panthers—a subspecies of the animal that is also called cougar, puma, and mountain lion—were alive by the 1980s. Their range has been ever more closely hemmed in over the past century by human encroachment. Field observations supported the view that their problem was just lack of suitable food.

But early DNA analysis found something else: the accumulating influence of inbreeding depression in the tiny population. Recessive traits such as kinked tails and cowlicks showed up more and more often, for example.

The population had long since been declared an endangered

species whose management was shared by an array of federal and state agencies. This complicated the decision making, especially when the relative importance of the genetics was in doubt. "Basically we documented an extinction in progress," veterinary scientist Melody Roelke-Parker of the National Cancer Institute says, "and I had extreme struggles trying to convince field people that there was something bad about this inbreeding. The consensus at the time was, 'Well, no other wild species has been documented to have problems.' All, I could say was: 'Pay attention. You're watching it.'"

Research began to clinch the case. By the early 1990s, 90 percent of the males only had one descended testicle, a few had none, and the sperm they produced was "just absolutely horrible," she says. "The worst-quality sperm of any mammal yet examined on this planet. The males had 5 percent normal sperm. It's quite amazing that they were able to keep making babies." She also discovered severe heart defects, an inbred trait that posed yet another immediate threat to the panthers.

More research data came through that also argued for adding to the Florida gene pool. DNA comparisons found that North American panthers are all so closely related that they may be a single subspecies. Moreover, the comparisons proved that the Florida group had historically interbred with populations in Texas before human settlement isolated them. That tended to moot the arguments against mixing genetically distinct populations.

So in 1995, eight Texas female panthers were introduced to the Floridians, and five ultimately bred. Reproduction has surged. Kinked tails, heart defects, and undescended testicles have all but disappeared among the three dozen Texas/Florida offspring so far. These "kittens"—some of them are now parents themselves—are feisty, too.

Panthers used to cower in surrender when treed and darted by biologists, National Park Service wildlife biologist Oron Bass says. But the "mixed" panthers will often leap from the branches high in a tree, out over the heads of dogs and biologists, and climb another tree or two—sometimes even after they are darted with tranquilizers. "If one of our objectives was to have a genetically vigorous animal, well then I'd say we have one," Bass has concluded.

Shoot, Poison, or Ingest

The new conservation genetics could also prove useful in the battle against invasive species in natural areas. Imagine gypsy moths, kudzu, or chestnut blight subdued by the introduction of genetically modified, sterile supercompetitors.

Researchers are quick to say that their studies of invasives so far suggest far more modest applications of the novel genetic techniques. But invasive species are regrettably abundant, and multiplying fast.

One such pest under scrutiny is the cowbird, an edge-dweller whose range expands as North American forests are fragmented by human development. Cowbirds are nest parasites: they destroy the eggs of other species and deposit their own, which are then nurtured by the host birds. Their role in wiping out populations of songbirds such as wood thrush that migrate to and from Latin America is well documented. With an eye toward controlling cowbird populations more effectively in the future, graduate student Bill Strausberger, under Mary Ashley's supervision at the University of Illinois, has attempted to decipher cowbird behavior.

"Although our work may not result directly in obvious management plans, what we learn should help guide management in some ways," Ashley says. No one knows how fecund the cowbird female is, for example. Using DNA tests to identify all the eggs of females over the course of a breeding season will show how often they reproduce.

Another question for would-be cowbird wranglers is whether females return to the same areas each year to parasitize nests. "Their fidelity to breeding areas will determine whether shooting them or poisoning them in a particular place will result in decreased rates of parasitism in subsequent years," Ashley says.

Another question whose answer might help get rid of the cowbird surplus: do individual females specialize, laying eggs in the nests of particular host species, or are they generalists, adapted to parasitize the nests of several different species? This can't be investigated without using genetics to link specific females with their eggs or chicks. If cowbirds do specialize, shooting or poisoning them in the nests of particular host species—say, the Kirtland's warbler—may offer effective protection for that species. But if the cowbirds are generalists, targeting the nests of Kirtland's warblers won't reduce the threat to that species.

Biologists are also groping for weapons to use against the introduced tamarisk, or salt cedar tree, which has taken over at least a million acres of U.S. riparian wetlands since its introduction from different regions of Eurasia in the 1800s. Its populations are said to be overtaking some forty thousand additional acres each year.

The tamarisk's big taproot pumps water from the margins of rivers, especially in the Southwest, lowering the water table. It concentrates salt on the surface of its leaves, and when they fall, the soil becomes so salty that nearly all other plant life vanishes.

Burning and herbicides can't eradicate tamarisk, and bulldozers, which can, are unwelcome in a fragile ecosystem. Geneticist Barbara Schaal of Washington University, St. Louis, calls it the plant from hell. The tamarisk is sparse in its native Eurasian habitats, "but when it comes over here it goes absolutely crazy," she says. This suggests some unexplained inhibiting factors in its native regions.

John Gaskin, a graduate student in Schaal's lab, is comparing tamarisk DNA from U.S. sites with samples he has gathered from Kazakhstan, Georgia, Iran, and China, where the U.S. populations originated.

"The idea is to find the source of origin so you can go out

there and find out what eats the damn plant," Schaal says.
"Then you can bring it to the U.S. and begin to test it as a biocontrol agent."

A far more aggressive kind of biocontrol would use genetics
to disrupt breeding in invasive species. Research is already under way to test genetically modified insects and microorganisms for use in agriculture and human health applications: a
pink cotton bollworm moth that passes fatal genes to its offspring might be a great boon to cotton farmers; a malaria-free
mosquito; a fix for the insect species—"kissing bugs"—that is
a vector for the dread Chagas' disease among humans in the
tropics.

The perils of brandishing biotechnology against invasives
are plain enough to all but the least wary. Says Joshua Ginsberg, director of the Wildlife Conservation Society's Asia program: "We just have to recognize that if you do stuff that
affects mammals and you get it wrong, well, we're mammals.
If it affects primates—we're primates!"

Conservation
Genetics II

Saving the sperm, ova, and DNA of rare animals in long-term cold storage banks, in the hope of reproducing the animals later, isn't science fiction. It's not even new—the San Diego Zoo started doing it thirty years ago. But the pace is picking up, as more such banks have opened in several countries lately—most recently at the American Museum of Natural History in New York.

Where some researchers see cold storage, though, others imagine a "frozen zoo." The use of the term exemplifies, for critics, the false promise of high-tech genetics in helping to ease the planetwide crisis of vanishing biological diversity.

The most mediagenic research of this kind tries to reproduce rare or even extinct species with cloning and other biotech feats. Those efforts, of which there are still very few, are either out in front or out in left field, depending on who's talking.

Advanced Cell Technology, Inc. (ACT), a private bioengineering firm in Worcester, Massachusetts, recently announced the birth of the first cloned endangered animal. The infant gaur, an increasingly rare humpbacked Asian wild ox, had been cloned from tissue provided by the San Diego Zoo and carried to term by a domestic cow.

The cloning was achieved by fusing a cow egg, from which the chromosomes had been stripped, with a long-dead gaur's skin cell and its DNA. The birth was only the latest chapter in the development of assisted reproduction techniques that include artificial insemination, in vitro fertilization, cross-species nuclear transfer, and cryopreservation of sperm, embryos, and cell tissue.

The cloned gaur, the much-publicized "Noah," died of an infection in less than two days. It was suspected that bacterial disease agents might have been tracked into Noah's pen by a film crew documenting the story. Despite the setback, the experiment was pronounced a success, at least by its sponsors.

Robert Lanza, M.D., an ACT vice president, told a reporter: "It's not science fiction. It's real. One hundred species are lost every day, and these mass extinctions are mostly our own doing. Now that we have the technology to reverse that, I think we have the responsibility to try."

But many conservation biologists object that it is, indeed, science fiction to suggest that cloning holds any broad promise for averting extinctions. They cringe at the potential take-home message for the public and for potential sources of funds for conservation projects: Humankind is off the hook, because high technology—not efforts to protect habitat—will save endangered species.

It's a conclusion that even the more ardent practitioners of cloning and frozen zookeeping disavow, however. Saved habitat protects hundreds of thousands of species, from rhinos to microorganisms. Then the animals themselves can do the work of maintaining their bafflingly complex, highly evolved relationships to the land and to each other, on into the indefinite future. Clone a picturesque animal, even an endangered one, and you have achieved far less.

But the tendency to blur the difference between a few captive animals and a whole ecosystem is not hard to find, among scientists and citizens alike.

EXTINCTION COULD BE A THING OF THE PAST was the headline on the gaur story in a London newspaper. "It could be the beginning of a new hope for some other endangered species—and, amazingly, even for some that are already extinct," the *Boston Globe* reported.

In India, the gaur and dozens of other threatened species are under accelerating pressure from habitat loss. The *Hindu*, one of the nation's largest-circulation dailies, announced:

WILD ANIMALS FOR THE ASKING!
Want a tiger, a leopard or a lion? Or any animal for that matter. Place a requisition and animals of your choice would be delivered.
Sounds incredible, but with the Laboratory for Conservation of Endangered Species all set to come up in the city, the prospect does not seem very distant.

"Once these banks are in place, we would be able to rejuvenate an animal species that is endangered or even resurrect one that goes extinct," says Dr. S. Shivaji, CCMB deputy director.

The gaur birth also moved the *Washington Post* to elated prose: "Noah's fetal heartbeat heralds the beginning of a new era of wildlife conservation in which endangered and even recently extinct animals may make dramatic comebacks through cloning techniques."

And in Sacramento, California, a letter to the editor: "Instead of those . . . environmental groups continually dividing people and jamming the courts over so-called endangered species, why don't they just save everybody a lot of headaches and use all that money on cloning?"

ACT head scientist Philip Damiani and others defend their work as forward-looking, and sometimes misunderstood. "We are not trying to produce identical offspring," he says, "but to use them in collaboration with captive breeding programs to salvage genetics that would be potentially lost. Sometimes animals die in zoos before they have a chance to breed, and their genetic line and value are lost. We're not trying to get rid of natural breeding programs, we are just trying to give them a hand up."

The gaur project "was pretty much done out of goodwill," Damiani explains. "The public perceives cloning as this horrible way of doing things. We actually saw people who criticized some of our previous work take a step back and say, 'Hey, we never thought you could apply it to this type of work.'"

Wild gaurs are disappearing because of hunting and loss of habitat to agricultural uses, Damiani says. Now is the time to learn how to sustain captive populations by preserving their genetic diversity. "Why wait until these animals get so low in numbers, like the pandas, that they become a dead-end species?" he asks.

Kurt Benirschke, recently retired president of the San Diego Zoo and an originator of freezing animal cell lines for scientific inquiry, aided the gaur cloning project. He says he has no doubt that cloning will "ultimately be useful for the reinsertion of genotypes that have become extinct," at least for zoo populations. The gaur experiment was "not for the heck of it," he says. "We wanted to answer some very specific questions. A lot of effort went into seeing whether embryonic transfer of a nucleus into a foreign genome would work."

Betsy Dresser, one of the stronger advocates of the "frozen zoo" concept, was the first researcher to transfer the thawed embryo of an endangered animal—an African wildcat—into another species, a domestic cat. Dresser's lab at the Audubon Center for Research of Endangered Species in New Orleans also plans to conduct cloning experiments.

"We don't know what the technologies are going to be like in the future," Dresser says. "If you consider dinosaurs and animals that have gone extinct, if we had properly frozen DNA from those animals we could revive them. The same thing exists today for elephants and rhinos and tigers and animals that are really going down in numbers. What we're focused on is being darn sure the DNA that we freeze, we know how to use, we know how to thaw, and we know that we can produce babies. For us it provides a future for species by keeping them from going extinct."

Cloning and cold storage are not panaceas for saving endangered species, Dresser says, but she advises critics to "Take it a hundred years forward. God knows what kind of technologies are going to be there and where we'll be. . . . This world is going to be so full of people, and it's going to crowd out every other species because we are so dominant.

"You know, what if we do go on to re-create life on other planets? It may sound very far-fetched now, but a hundred years from now it may be just run-of-the-mill." She is working on a book entitled *Tigers to the Moon*.

Irrelevant

Critics among conservation biologists have strong misgivings about talk of cloning and frozen zoos, however. Here are a few:

Despite their dazzle, these are time-consuming, expensive, and failure-prone procedures. In all but a few extreme cases, endangered species themselves are able to reproduce far more effectively and easily on their own.

Even when assisted reproduction works, reintroducing animals to the wild poses a very high hurdle. A study by Benjamin Beck, associate director for animal programs at the Smithsonian's National Zoo, concluded that as few as 11 percent of documented reintroductions may have succeeded. The animals do not know how to forage, avoid predators, or migrate, and there is usually no way to teach them.

"What do you do with the animal once you've cloned him?" asks Joshua Ginsberg, head of the Wildlife Conservation Society's Asia program. "You get pandas that don't know how to be pandas."

Cloned animals, including Dolly the sheep, often turn out to have major physiological defects, such as deformed hearts or lungs, obesity, or developmental abnormalities.

"It's difficult for me to imagine very many situations where cloning technology would be useful—where that would be a good use of our resources," says geneticist George Amato. "Because if a species is in that plight it might in a sense be past its time. You might want to devote your efforts to problems where you have a greater likelihood of being successful."

Conservation biologist Stuart Pimm of Columbia University acknowledges that genetics is crucial in some endangered species recovery projects. But he dismisses the implied promise of the term "frozen zoo"—that preserved cells may be a lifeline. "It's not a solution," Pimm says. "It's not even a hint of a solution. It's a sideshow of a sideshow of a sideshow. Nothing exemplifies the problem more than the pandas. The Chinese now have a captive breeding facility, so you can go and see a bunch of pandas munching away on bamboo. But the reserve is losing three hundred hectares of panda habitat every year, an appalling rate. The idea that you're going to save pandas by doing genetic modifications is just nonsense. You're going to save pandas by protecting habitat, and the habitat has not been protected."

Meanwhile, he worries, the millions of dollars needed to work out effective habitat protection measures for threatened species may be diverted to elaborate research, infrastructure, overhead, and marginal experiments. "It's not benignly irrelevant. It's malevolently irrelevant," Pimm says.

David Wildt, a reproduction biologist at the National Zoo's Conservation and Research Center in Front Royal, Virginia, has used assisted reproduction to aid breeding in a long, patient, and to date successful program to reintroduce black-footed ferrets to their former habitat in the western United States. They were once thought to be extinct.

He has called for a network of cold storage genome resource banks as a limited hedge against loss of genetic variation in the future. But he decries the term "frozen zoo" and is disturbed by some of the high-tech hopes of scientists and the public.

"It takes away from the higher priority, which is the need for funding basic studies to simply understand the fundamental reproductive biology of species like the gaur," Wildt says. Of the forty thousand vertebrate species on Earth, only a hundred have been studied adequately in terms of reproductive biology, he adds. "Everyone simply believes the technology can be used to save endangered species. Well, that's really not the case."

Puzzle Pieces

"The secret," says Betsy Dresser, "is for all of us to do what we do best—saving habitat, running zoos, doing laboratory research to do cloning or assisted reproduction. Informed partnerships—so that all of us are doing simultaneously what we do best. In my mind, that's the only way we are going to save wildlife."

It's a sentiment few seem to take issue with, except to lay the strongest possible emphasis on "informed partnerships." If advances in genetics and reproductive technology are to be useful, they'll have to be integrated into the rest of conservation biology to confront "holistic kinds of problems," Wildt says.

"If it's not done in the context of a management plan, or a recovery program, or working with the managers of other disciplines, it's just a gee-whiz kind of event," he adds. "Those so-called milestones rarely show up in the scientific literature. They show up in the *Washington Post* or on the *Today* show."

High-tech aside, reproductive biologists alone can't get the job done, Wildt argues. In a forthcoming anthology to which he has contributed, a schematic "conservation puzzle" is pictured. Each of the thirteen interlocking puzzle pieces is labeled with a discipline such as population biology, sociology, or endocrinology that is necessary for successful species conservation. One is labeled "luck." "It all has to do with interdisciplinary research and working together," he says.

For conservation genetics in general, Amato, too, has issued a call to better integration among disciplines. "What we need to do," he told participants in the New York symposium, "is move towards a greater integration of research and synthesis with the other disciplines of conservation biology and conservation management." And he cautioned colleagues to "avoid letting the press and public's fascination with genetic manipulation lead to a false sense of optimism and hope for a technological solution to this extinction crisis. . . . The overriding message is that context and connection is the necessary framework."

Index

Ogden, Jim, 59–60
Ohio State University, 24
oil drilling, coast of Florida, 3
oil spill, on Caribbean coast, 2–3
old-forest ecosystems, 31–33
old-growth forests, 27–46
Olin, James R. (D-Va.), 63
olive-sided flycatcher, 83
organic matter recycling, 95
Orr, David, 60
Overcash, Jesse, 27–29, 45–46

Pacific Northwest, 28
Palumbi, Stephen, 141
pandas, 154
panthers: Florida panther, 144–
  46; mixed breeding of, 145–
  46; population estimates, 4
Pardieck, Keith, 87
Pea Ridge, Arkansas, 52
Pearson, Les, 133, 136
Petersburg, Virginia, battlefield,
  60
Peter's Mountain mallow, 89–92
Peterson, Rolf, 68–70, 71, 73–
  74, 76
Pilot Knob, Missouri, 52
Piltz, Rick S., 6–8
Pimental, David, 100
Pimm, Stuart, 154
pit and mound topography, 32
Plant Protection Act, 113
political interference in
  scientific research, 2, 4–5
pollinating insects, value of,
  95–96
population growth, and plant
  remains, 24
Potomac-Garrett State Forest,
  Maryland, 41

Powell, William, 138
predator-prey interaction,
  77–80, 95; edge-dwelling
  predators, 36; genetic
  engineering, effect of on, 131
President's National Medal of
  Science, 38
Prodigene, 133
Prospero, Ming Lee, 93
public education as protection
  for insects, 97–98
Public Employees for
  Environmental Responsibility
  (PEER), 4
Public Interest Research
  Group, 38

Rabenoid, Kerry, 83, 84
Raffa, Kenneth, 131, 135
Randall, John, 89–90
RAND Corporation, 101
Rappole, John, 85, 86, 87
rare species management, 141–48
Raven, Peter, 38
Reaser, Jamie, 100, 108
Rey, Mark, 39, 106
Robbins, Chandler, 36
Roberts, David L., 108–9
Robinson, Scott, 85
Roelke-Parker, Melody, 145
Roger Williams Park Zoo, Rhode
  Island, 93

salmon, 119
Salt Creek tiger beetle, 98
Samson, Douglas, 36
San Diego Zoo, 149
Savage River, Maryland, 38
Schaal, Barbara, 147–48
Scott, Douglas, 51–52